P9-DTA-161

FENG SHUI

WORKBOOK

THE FENG SHUI WORK BOOK

A room-by-room guide
to effective feng shui
in your home and workplace

WU XING

The members of Wu Xing are:
Joanne O'Brien
Martin Palmer
Zhao Xiaomin
Landform Adviser: Eva Wong

Illustrated by Meilo So

TUTTLE

Charles E. Tuttle Co., Inc.
Boston • Rutland, Vermont • Tokyo

NOTE TO THE READER

This book is an interpretation of traditional Chinese beliefs, and their value and truth should be judged at your discretion. Common sense is needed in the application of feng shui and the authors, packager and publisher cannot be held responsible for accident or injury to persons or property resulting from its use.

First published in 1998 by Tuttle Publishing, an imprint of Periplus Editions (HK) Ltd., with editorial offices at 153 Milk Street, Boston, Massachusetts 02109.

Text copyright © ICOREC 1998
Illustrations copyright © Meilo So/The Artworks 1998
This edition copyright © Eddison Sadd Editions 1998

The right of Joanne O'Brien, Martin Palmer, Zhao Xiaomin and Eva Wong, representing the Wu Xing feng shui consultancy group, to be identified as the authors of this work has been asserted by them in accordance with the British Copyright, Design and Patents Act 1988.

All rights reserved. No part of this publication may be reproduced or utilized in any form or by any means, electronic or mechanical, including photocopying, recording, or by any information storage and retrieval system, without prior written permission from Tuttle Publishing.

The Library of Congress Catalog Card Number: 98-60074

Distributed by

Charles E. Tuttle Co., Inc.
RR1 Box 231-5
North Clarendon,
VT 05759
Tel: (802) 773-8930
Fax: (802) 773-6993

Tuttle Shokai Ltd.
1-21-13, Seki
Tama-ku, Kawasaki-shi 214
Japan
Tel: (044) 833-0225
Fax: (044) 822-0413

First Edition
05 04 03 02 01 00 99 98   1 3 5 7 9 10 8 6 4 2

AN EDDISON·SADD EDITION
Edited, designed and produced by
Eddison Sadd Editions Limited
St Chad's House, 148 King's Cross Road
London WC1X 9DH

Phototypeset in Berkeley and Baker Signet using QuarkXPress on Apple Macintosh
Origination by Atlas Mediacom (S) Pte Ltd, Singapore
Printed and bound by Bath Press Colourbooks, Glasgow, Great Britain

Contents

Introduction 6

PART ONE: YOUR FENG SHUI TOOLS 8
The Principles of Feng Shui 10
The Five Elements 20
The Pa Tzu Compass 24
Feng Shui Solutions: Protecting a Site 28

PART TWO: IMPROVING YOUR FENG SHUI 34
How to Use Part Two 36

OUTSIDE THE HOME 38
Mountains, Hills and Rivers 40 • Feng Shui in Rural Landscapes 45
Road Patterns 49

FEATURES AROUND THE HOME 54
Houses in Relation to Other Buildings 56 • Plots of Land 60 • Gardens 64
The Shape of Your Home 68 • The Front Door 73

INSIDE THE HOME 78
How to Analyse Your Apartment Floor Plan 80 • The Hall and Stairs 82
The Living Room 84 • The Kitchen 90 • The Bedroom 96
The Bathroom 102 • The Dining Room 104

IN THE WORKPLACE 106
How to Analyse Your Office Floor Plan 108 • The Site of a Business 110
Entrance to the Workplace 118 • Lobbies, Corridors and Doors 120
Workplace Layout 122

Bibliography and Further Reading 126
Index 126
Acknowledgements 128

Introduction

Ch'i cannot be seen or heard but its influence can be found in all things, from the flow of a river to the peak of a mountain, and from a thriving shopping centre to a quiet suburban street. *Ch'i* is the 'life breath', or energy, that is continually gathering and dispersing, rising and falling, condensing and evaporating. *Feng shui* (pronounced 'fung shway') is the art of understanding the flow of ch'i, of recognizing hidden forces in the land and in the cosmos – forces that may be in perfect harmony in one place but in complete disarray in another.

Feng shui is also a way of looking at our environment that will be unfamiliar to many in the West: landforms are not simply static sites upon which we express our designs or needs, but are forms shaped by the flow of energy – forms that influence all life around them.

Feng shui is an ancient Chinese term that means 'wind and water'. These are the elemental forces that shape and mould the landscape, seen in the movement of ch'i and the balance of yin and yang. All things in the universe are in a constant state of change, and yin and yang are the expression of this change. Yin is powerful, strong, hot and fiery while yang is luminous, watery, cool and dark; they are present in all patterns, activities, forms and emotions. A skilled feng shui practitioner reads the movement of ch'i and understands the balance of yin and yang, and is able to see how they are expressed across the landscape and assess their influence on a particular site.

Feng shui hinges on the belief that we recognize the existence of an intrinsic harmony, but that in certain places this harmony is disjointed or broken. Once the source of the problem has been identified, corrective measures can be taken to try to re-establish balance. Instead of being passive recipients we take an active and cooperative role in the workings of the world around us.

Using the Workbook

This easy-to-follow workbook explains the principles that govern feng shui and shows you how to 'read' and understand your environment. It provides an essential guide to rural and urban landscapes that gives you the opportunity to assess important features both in and around your home and workplace, as well as to take appropriate steps to improve the feng shui where needed.

Part One introduces the philosophy of feng shui, beginning with the Tao, which is regarded as the ultimate source of all life. The forces of yin and yang and the energy of ch'i, so central to the practice of feng shui, arise from the harmony of the Tao and are described here to enable you to read their balance and effect in a particular area.

The process of change that is seen in the movement of yin and yang is represented by the eight trigrams of the *I Ching*, the ancient Chinese oracle that dates back thousands of years. Each trigram is associated with a direction of the compass as well as one of the five Chinese elements: this system provides the basis for your personal *Pa Tzu* compass readings which you can use to ensure that the elements are harmonious in your home. This early section of the book also introduces you to the idea of looking at the land as a dynamic and animate force endowed with beneficial or destructive qualities. In feng shui, the energy present in the land and water is reflected in the form of a dragon, and the qualities the dragon bestows upon natural features are also explored here. Many feng shui 'problems' observed at a site can be resolved by implementing simple measures, and so this section includes general 'solutions'. These are the guidelines to using countermeasures to control the flow of ch'i or protect against destructive energy.

Once armed with your 'tools' – an understanding of how feng shui works, how to assess your environment and use your Pa Tzu compass, and how to make improvements – you are ready to move on to the practical section.

Part Two shows you – step by step – how to carry out readings for every aspect of your surroundings, from the location of your home to the layout of your living-room furniture. This highly visual section illustrates both positive and negative examples throughout, and offers easy-to-follow advice whenever improvements are needed. So, starting from the outside and working in, we move from the rural landscape to road patterns, shape and position of buildings, plots of land, gardens and the entrance to a house or building. Once inside the home, you begin by assessing the overall layout and then working through each room in turn. Whether you want to check the size and position of furniture, doors and windows, or find out if your colour scheme is in harmony with your personal element, there is something here to cater for everyone. Checklists offer helpful reminders of what to look out for in each room. And there is also advice on how to improve feng shui in the workplace, however limited the scope for improvement may be.

Whatever your situation, this indispensable guide shows you how feng shui can help you to change your life.

wisdom

Your Feng Shui Tools

This section introduces the principles of feng shui, explaining how it works and how to read feng shui in your environment. You can discover how to balance the five elements to establish harmony in your home, and calculate your personal Pa Tzu compass to find out your lucky and unlucky directions. General 'remedies' that you can use to improve feng shui are also included in this section. Together, these are the 'tools' you will be putting to practical use when you come to assess your surroundings in Part Two.

The Principles of Feng Shui

The Tao

At its heart feng shui is a way of working with the natural harmony, or order, of the universe – the Tao. The Tao is often translated as the Way or Path, a path that has been followed for centuries by sages and immortals. But the Tao has a more profound meaning – it is the ultimate source of all life (see extract below left).

The Tao is the origin of all things that existed before creation. Although its ultimate nature is beyond form and language, the Tao is visibly expressed in the pattern of nature and the interdependency of all living things. Feng shui is a way of expressing our relationship with the Tao, a guide to living in harmony with this primordial energy. Through feng shui our relationship with the environment is not one of control or dominance but rather one of interrelationship.

The patterns of change in the seasons, in the landscape and also in our emotions reflect the movement of the Tao. Just as a bright day may become overcast or a storm gives way to stillness, positive and negative aspects rise and fall: nothing is created or exists in isolation. Life flourishes, then decays to return to the Tao and in the process of decay new life arises. Feng shui is a way of reading this process of change, of identifying areas of life-giving or decaying energy and actively balancing elements and correcting weaknesses.

Heaven, Earth and Humanity

The triad of heaven, earth and humanity is the classic expression of the Tao, and is frequently represented in Chinese landscape paintings. Towering mountain peaks, often shrouded in clouds, reach up to the sky, symbolizing the union of heaven and earth. Steep slopes are balanced by a gentler, greener landscape where water and land meet, a sign of flourishing earth energy. Scattered across the landscape are signs of human dwellings, people fishing, farming or simply travelling along the mountain paths. The houses and temples blend harmoniously with the landscape, protected by its forms, completing the balance between heaven, earth and humanity.

The Tao gives birth to the One
The One gives birth to the Two
The Two gives birth to the Three
The Three gives birth to every living thing.

All things are held in yin, and carry yang:
And they are held together in the ch'i of
teeming energy.

(Chapter 42, *The Illustrated Tao Te Ching,*
Man-Ho Kwok, Martin Palmer and Jay Ramsay)

Humanity is schooled by the Earth
Earth is taught by Heaven
And Heaven is guided by the Tao

And the Tao goes with what is
absolutely natural.

(Chapter 25, *The Illustrated Tao Te Ching,*
Man-Ho Kwok, Martin Palmer and Jay Ramsay)

Yin and Yang

Yin and yang are natural forces that are present in all life, continually rising and falling, expanding or withdrawing. Yin and yang are in constant state of movement and through this dynamic interplay they create the changing pattern of life. Their interaction is clearly seen in the cycle of the seasons: yang is at its peak in the heat of summer while yin is at its weakest. As autumn mists appear yin begins its ascendency while yang starts to decline; by midwinter yang has withdrawn while yin is powerful, but with the increasing warmth of spring yang begins to expand once again.

Yin and yang are said to have been created at the beginning of time when everything was vague and formless. First, the universe was created out of this emptiness, and in its turn the universe created clear, light forces that drifted up to become heaven, while the heavy forces solidified to form the earth. According to the writings of Huai Nan Tzu (c. 120 BC):

ABOVE *The well-known yin/yang symbol represents the ever-changing patterns of life.*

The union of heaven, earth and humanity can be found in a classic Chinese landscape: the mountains soar skywards while human activity flourishes below.

'The combined essences of heaven and earth became yin and yang, the concentrated essences of yin and yang became the four seasons, and the scattered essences of the four seasons became the myriad creatures of the world. After a long time the hot forces of the accumulated yang produced fire and the essence of the fire force became the sun; the cold force of accumulated yin became water and the essence of the water force became the moon. The essence of the excess force of the sun and moon became the stars and planets. Heaven received the sun, moon and stars while earth received water and soil.'

(*Huai Nan Tzu,* quoted in *Sources of Chinese Tradition Vol. I,* edited by Theodore de Bary)

Yin and yang are most commonly described as opposite, dynamic forces: yang is male and yin is female, yang is hot and yin is cold, yang is anger and yin is withdrawal, yang is activity and yin is stillness, yang is sharp and yin is soft.

In feng shui, however, yin and yang take on an additional and different dimension. The landscape in feng shui is categorized as land or water: land is still and yin, whereas water is active and yang, which is why the ideal site combines hills and rivers. These two categories of the yin mountain and yang water are further subdivided according to the nature of the mountain – steep or gently undulating – or the nature of the water – stormy or still.

For example, craggy peaks are yin but flat-topped mountains are yang, and steep cliffs are yin but gentle slopes are yang. The yang aspects are more productive and dynamic while the yin aspects can be dangerous or destructive. Still water gathers energy and is yang but fast-flowing water disperses energy and is yin; rivers that follow an irregular and sharply turning course are yin but an evenly flowing meandering river is yang since it produces positive energy. When water spurts out of the earth it is yin but it is yang when it seeps into the earth to nourish underground streams. Nothing is completely yin or yang since these forces continually interact, thus there is always an element of yin in yang and yang in yin.

This dynamic relationship is central to feng shui, and an understanding of yin and yang is vital if you are to make a true assessment of your surroundings.

A site where steep cliffs meet stormy waters is powerfully yin. The energy here is destructive and you would be advised against choosing to live in this location.

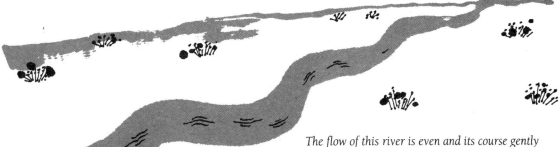

The flow of this river is even and its course gently meanders to produce positive yang energy. However, the surrounding land is relatively flat and featureless, making it a potential source of negative, yin energy.

Ch'i

'Throughout heaven and earth there is Li and there is Ch'i. Li is the Tao organizing all forms from above, and root from which all things are produced. Ch'i is the instrument composing all forms from below, and the tools and raw materials by which all things are made.'

(The Collected Works of Chu Hsi from *Science and Civilisation in China Vol. II*, translated by J. Needham)

Ch'i is the life-giving breath or energy that shapes and animates all life. It is continually moving and changing – the places where it gathers produce positive energy and the sites where it disperses allow negative energy to settle. Ch'i can be channelled to condense at a particular place, thereby enhancing the site's fortune, but if there is no room for movement it will become trapped. In an open featureless area there is nothing to hold ch'i, and so it sweeps across the land and soon evaporates. At a more detailed level, the flow of ch'i can be blocked by a piece of furniture or quickly escape through an open door. In most cases, however, ch'i flow can be regulated and controlled to prevent negative forces draining away the life energy.

In addition to the ch'i that courses through the land and rivers, and the ch'i that accumulates and disperses at certain points on the ground, there is also heaven ch'i. This is the ch'i that governs the cycle of the seasons and is closely identified with yin and yang. Heaven ch'i is divided into twenty-four phases, which mark the climatic and agricultural patterns of the year. The first phase is *Li Ch'un* – Beginning of Spring – a time when yin is declining and yang is ascending. The middle of the year is marked by *Ta Shu* – Great Heat – when yang is at its peak, and the year ends at *Ta Han* – Great Cold – when yin is at its most powerful.

Sha: The Life-taking Breaths

Ch'i that flows through and over the land is also subject to weakness and decay. When it is dispersed or blocked its positive energy is drained and *sha* or life-taking breaths are allowed to enter. Sha produces negative or destructive energy – for example, the accumulation of refuse is a source of sha, as is stagnant water or rotting vegetation. Sha is also felt in bitterly cold winds that pierce gaps between buildings, or in the lightning forks of violent storms. It can travel along straight lines such as electric power cables, arrow-like roads and railway lines, or can be directed from the sharp corner of a building or natural feature. In most instances, corrective action can be taken to remove, block or deflect the source of sha, thereby allowing ch'i to re-establish itself.

The Trigrams

The continual interaction and tension between yin and yang creates the pattern of movement and change in the universe – a pattern ordained by the Tao. This never-ending cycle is reflected in the eight trigrams of the I Ching. Each trigram is made up of three lines, which can be broken (a yin line) or unbroken (a yang line). One trigram has yin lines only, while another has yang only; the remainder are a mixture of yin and yang. They are ordered in a circle to reflect the gradual movement from absolute yin to absolute yang, and back to absolute yin in a continuous cycle (*see right*).

If you look at the main Pa Tzu compass on page 24 you will see the eight trigrams positioned in their circular formation, each trigram relating to a particular element and direction. The order the trigrams follow is known as the Later Heaven sequence, and this is the order used on traditional feng shui compasses to show the balance and movement of yin and yang on the ground. (There is another sequence known as Former Heaven, which follows a different order representing the annual cycle of yin and yang through the seasons; this sequence is a reflection of the cosmic forces of yin and yang.)

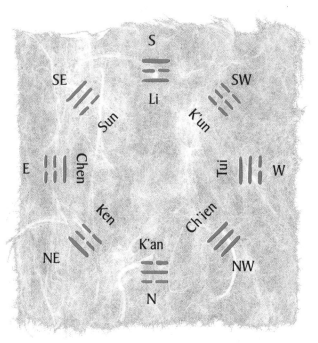

The top line of the trigrams is on the outside and the lower line on the inside. South is at the top of this sequence since Chinese compasses are orientated south–north.

The trigrams have universal associations, including natural phenomena and attributes, among other things, and some of these are listed below.

The Trigram Associations

	Trigram	Direction	Natural Phenomenon	Attributes	Member of Family
	Li	south	fire	adherence, dependence	middle daughter
	K'un	south-west	earth	receptive, yielding	mother
	Tui	west	lake	joy, serenity	youngest daughter
	Ch'ien	north-west	heaven	creative, strong	father
	K'an	north	water	danger, flowing water	middle son
	Ken	north-east	mountain	steadiness, stillness	youngest son
	Chen	east	thunder	arousing movement	eldest son
	Sun	south-east	wind	penetration, gentleness	eldest daughter

The Five Elements

The five elements of wood, fire, earth, metal and water are used in traditional Chinese arts to describe the process of change. They exist to a greater or lesser extent in all substances and their interaction illustrates the continual growth and decay within the universe. According to the *Shu Ching*, or Book of History, Heaven decreed the order of the universe and the first plan was to divide all phenomena into five elements:

> 'The nature of water is to soak and descend; of fire, to blaze and ascend; of wood, to be crooked and to be straight; of metal to obey and to change; while the virtue of earth is seen in seed-sowing and ingathering. That which soaks and descends becomes salt; that which blazes and ascends becomes bitter; that which is crooked and straight becomes sour; that which obeys and changes becomes acrid; and from seed-sowing and ingathering becomes sweetness.'
>
> (*The Great Plan*, from *The Chinese Classics Vol. III*, translated by James Legge)

The elements exist in a continual cycle of creation and destruction: some create, feed and strengthen, while others weaken, dissipate and destroy. This is a necessary process, however, since each interaction gives rise to a new element. The flux and opposition of yin and yang are also seen in their movement: for example, when the element of water is stagnant it is yin, when it is clean and flowing smoothly it is yang, and when it is stormy and dangerous it is once again yin. The effect of the interaction of the elements and how to interpret them in a reading is discussed further on pages 20–3.

The Dragon

In feng shui practice, the shapes of the land, the flow of rivers and the patterns created by light and wind are associated with a variety of animal forms. These animals bestow a quality on the land that can be dynamic, energetic or dangerous. Of all the animals, however, the dragon is the most important landform, identifiable in virtually every topographical feature. It is seen in linear shapes, and ridges, hilltops, slopes, hills and valleys are all veins of the dragon and the source of the dragon's breath. The ch'i that courses through the land is known as the dragon's blood. The dragon is also seen in the pattern of watercourses, when it is known

The dragon is identified in the shape of the land, and the ch'i that flows over and through the land is known as the dragon's blood.

as the Water Dragon: the rivers are the dragon's ducts along which ch'i is channelled (*see page 41*).

The dragon is, therefore, more than just a metaphor for mountains and rivers – it is actually an animate presence that carries life-giving energy. The dragon's veins vary from kingly to ordinary – from powerful majestic peaks, a range of mountain ridges and sweeping valleys to a small range of low rolling hills. The dragon's presence can be dangerous if the mountain ridges end abruptly and steeply since the ch'i cannot be absorbed gently into the land. The dragon's form should build up from scattered lower veins to higher peaks that stretch out to create a long spine, and then slowly scatter once again into lower ridges.

There are also many variations of the dragon's form; some hold dynamic energy for centuries giving them the ability to sustain repeated use, while others cannot regenerate once they have been used for building. Some dragon forms are deep and concentrated sources of energy; others are less intensive and their energy is diffused. (*See page 40 for examples of dynamic animal forms.*)

Often the power of a mountain is enhanced by water flowing across its veins. When water flows steadily towards a dynamic mountain the energies gather to generate great power – the mountain concentrates the water energy while the water spreads the mountain energy – but water flowing swiftly from a site will weaken and drain those energies.

As the water flows swiftly away from the site towards the sea, the dragon's energy is drained. The ch'i that was concentrated in the dragon's form on this mountain changes abruptly as it rolls forcefully down the steep cliffs.

Wind

Wind is another carrier of energy. Sharp cold winds cutting through cracks, blowing over ridges or racing across plains carry destructive energy, while gentle breezes animate and spread ch'i. Wind blowing across a mountain range sometimes travels like an arrow piercing gaps and valleys, but if the dragon's veins in the mountain are balanced they control the wind and channel it towards the site.

Sites on open hills or plains need protection from vegetation or buildings to control the impact of wind flow and protect the site. In contrast, a site that is completely overshadowed or enclosed could become a source of sha since there is no movement to activate ch'i. A balance has to be established so that the site is not vulnerable to adverse weather conditions yet is open enough to benefit from natural light and warmth.

Landform Energy

When a site is weak or vulnerable a large structure can help to balance or protect it, although obviously the structure will not have had the time to absorb the primordial energy of the universe that is an inherent part of most landforms. When mountains are levelled, valleys flooded or quarries built the deep source of energy that has been accumulated over millennia is cut, swept away or destroyed. Likewise, the construction of large-scale power stations or dams disturb, weaken and often destroy a dynamic site. When natural disasters occur, such as volcanic eruptions, earthquakes or landslides, the earth's energy is abruptly forced out and new landforms may result. Some may block the path of energy and others may channel energy effectively, although these new landforms have not had sufficient time to become deep sources of energy.

Although this house is isolated, the wind is channelled through the valleys towards the site at the centre and its flow is balanced by the protective hills around the site.

The Four Animal Guardians

Every site, whether urban or rural, is surrounded by four animal spirits: the Black Tortoise, Red Bird, Green Dragon and White Tiger. In its early history feng shui was developed to determine auspicious sites for burial so the spirits of the ancestors were calmed and protected. These four animals were the guardians around the grave and their position was – and still is – determined from the position of the grave itself looking outwards to the Red Bird, backed behind by the Black Tortoise, with the Green Dragon to the left and the White Tiger to the right. In feng shui, burial sites belong to the yin domain (*see below*).

The animal spirits that surround residential or commercial buildings are determined from a different perspective, since these buildings belong to the yang domain. When taking a reading the observer stands outside, facing towards the front of the building. The Red Bird is at the front of the site, the Black Tortoise at the back, the Green Dragon on the left and the White Tiger on the right (*see right*). The role of the four animal guardians in protecting rural sites is discussed further on page 40, and features throughout the book in relation to examples of good and bad feng shui sites.

RIGHT *The yang-domain animal formation applies to homes and businesses. This is the formation you will need to account for when you assess your surroundings.*

BELOW *The yin-domain animal formation is applied to burial sites to ensure that the spirits of the ancestors are protected and can rest peacefully.*

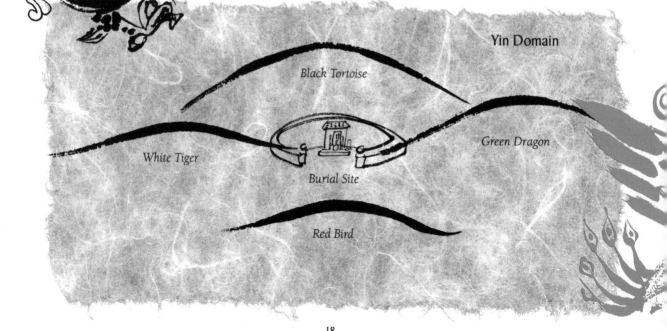

Yin Domain

Black Tortoise

Green Dragon

White Tiger

Burial Site

Red Bird

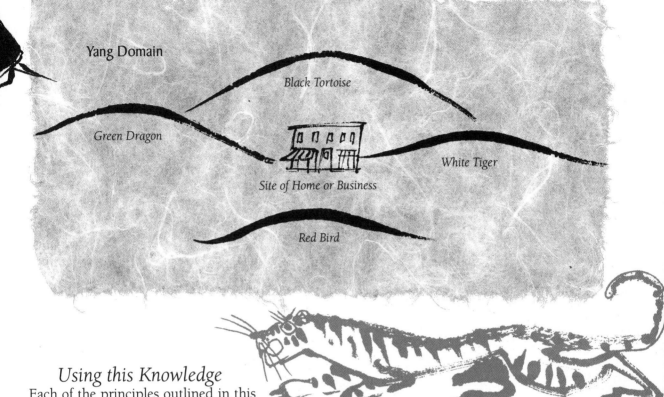

Yang Domain

Black Tortoise

Green Dragon

Site of Home or Business

White Tiger

Red Bird

Using this Knowledge

Each of the principles outlined in this section plays a role in building up an understanding of a site. In Part Two, a wide range of sites are illustrated that provide immediate guidance, but the information on feng shui principles gives you a deeper understanding of how and why these guidelines were created.

If you are carrying out a reading of a specific feature it cannot be taken in isolation from the surrounding environment. For example, the feng shui of a house is first of all affected by the site – is it on a hillside or in a valley, is it subject to powerful yin or yang forces, is it on a site where the dragon is powerful? If you live in an urban area, buildings often take the place of natural features, so taller buildings to the rear of a house, in the position of the Black Tortoise, offer the protection that a hill might provide in a rural area. Similarly, heavy and fast-moving traffic in front of your house will dissipate energy in the same way that the strong current of a fast-flowing river will disperse ch'i.

It is important to build up a picture that takes account of both large- and small-scale factors, since a strength in one area might help to offset a weakness in another. It is inevitable that some features simply cannot be changed, but you will find that it is always possible to use a variety of tools to create a more balanced and harmonious site.

The Five Elements

The Chinese call the five elements *wu xing*, *wu* meaning 'five' and *xing* meaning 'to go' or 'to move'. Although the five elements are classified as wood, fire, earth, metal and water, they are essentially a way of referring to the movements, actions and changes that take place at every level of life.

The elements are not static but are continually nourishing each other or overpowering one another. They are types of energy that shape and transform all life; as such, they are present in everything, although one element may be more dominant than the others. The elements are reflected in shapes, forms, textures, colours, directions, health and patterns of change, which is why they are important to understanding and practising feng shui. Also, when you come to analyse a floor plan of a room or a house you will need to be familiar with the elements in order to improve and strengthen a weak area.

The Cycles of the Elements

The interaction of the elements can be productive or destructive – some elements overpower each other and some produce each other. For example, when water is powerful it overwhelms and extinguishes fire, but if fire is powerful it reduces objects to ashes to produce earth. This process is summed up by saying water destroys fire and fire produces earth.

In this productive cycle, wood burns to produce heat and the upward movement of fire. Fire then consumes objects, turning them to ashes to produce earth. The nourishing quality of the earth produces metal and, in turn, the metal in the earth enriches underground water. Water rises to

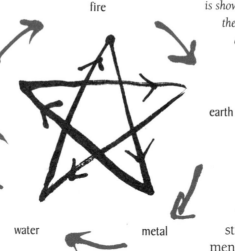

fire

wood

earth

water

metal

The productive cycle of the five elements is shown in the outer circle, while the inner pentagram shows the destructive cycle of the five elements.

the surface to feed vegetation thus to produce wood, and so the cycle of production continues (*see below*).

In this destructive cycle, wood covers and penetrates the earth, constricting and taking nourishment from it. In its turn, earth controls the direction and flow of streams and rivers. Water overcomes the flames and heat of fire and ultimately extinguishes it. Fire weakens and then melts metal, and the sharp, cutting power of metal can destroy wood (*see left*), thus beginning the cycle once more.

Productive cycle	Destructive cycle
wood produces fire	wood destroys earth
fire produces earth	earth destroys water
earth produces metal	water destroys fire
metal produces water	fire destroys metal
water produces wood	metal destroys wood

When you come to read the feng shui of a room or house using the Pa Tzu compass, it is important to know how these elements combine with each other. Every direction has an element associated with it and you also have your own personal element (which you will discover when you come to pages 24–7). You will need to know whether your element works in harmony with, or clashes with, the element of the particular direction you are assessing. If your element is harmonious you have a positive reading, but if it clashes you will need to improve the reading by following the suggested remedial methods.

Universal Associations

Over the centuries the elements have been linked with numerous features, such as planets, tastes, weather conditions, parts of the body, and domestic animals (*see below*). The system of matching the five elements has been developed to such an extent that they can be correlated to almost anything in the universe. Since the elements are at the heart of all the processes of change, their wide-ranging associations can be used in a variety of divinational and medicinal practices, from astrology through to Chinese herbal medicine.

Element Associations

Element	Planet	Taste	Weather	Organ	Animal
WOOD	Jupiter	sourness	wind	spleen	sheep
FIRE	Mars	bitterness	heat	lungs	poultry
EARTH	Saturn	sweetness	sunshine	heart	ox
METAL	Venus	acridity	cold	kidney	dog
WATER	Mercury	saltiness	rain	liver	pig

The Five Elements and Yin and Yang

The dynamic tension of yin and yang is also seen in the five elements. Yang is at its peak in the heat and light of fire, and although it is still relatively strong it is less powerful in the growth and productivity of wood. On the other hand, yin is at its peak in the cold and damp qualities of water, while it is strong but less dominant in the malleable qualities of metal. The forces of yin and yang are equally balanced and harmonious in the element of earth.

Using the Elements to Improve Your Feng Shui

When you come to analyse a floor plan of a room you may find that certain elements clash – one element may need to be strengthened or the overpowering one may need to be channelled in another direction. In order to improve your feng shui you need to know how to introduce, or diminish, each of the elements, and the colours and objects listed to the right will help you to do so.

For example, if the fire element is too powerful in your bedroom it could cause sleepless nights. First, you need to check how fire can be controlled according to the elemental cycles: fire produces earth; fire destroys metal; and water destroys fire.

The power of fire can be diminished by the element of water, so the introduction of a clear glass vase of flowers, a bowl of water or paintings of water scenes will weaken fire. You can also use the colour black in fabrics or ornaments, but do not overwhelm the room with black. Or you can weaken fire by directing it towards colours, textures and objects associated with earth: if the element of earth is increased, fire will be weakened as it works to feed and create earth. And, since fire destroys metal, the introduction of metal colours and objects will challenge and dissipate fire. However, do not let elements attack each other too forcefully when using the destructive cycle.

The elemental colours can be used in a variety of ways, from cushions, curtains, blinds, paint or wallpaper to furniture or ornaments. Rooms do not necessarily need to be dominated by one colour – often the introduction of that colour through one or two items will help to establish balance.

Element and Colour

WOOD can be shaped and formed and is associated with relaxation.

Colour: green. All shades of green can be used, from pale green through to lime green, sea green, mid-green and dark green.

FIRE has burning and ascending qualities and is associated with enlightenment.

Colour: red. Various shades ranging from deep orange and pink, through to fiery red, deep red, purple and burgundy can be used.

EARTH has productive and creative qualities and is associated with care and attention.

Colour: yellow. Colours ranging from light orange to pale lemon hues, and from bright yellow to a warm golden colour, can be used.

METAL has malleable qualities and is associated with energy.

Colour: white. Shades ranging from pale greys and off-white to brilliant white and cream can be used.

WATER has qualities of soaking and descending and is associated with peace and quiet.

Colour: black. Dark colours, such as dark grey, deep blue or indigo through to various hues of black, can be used.

How to Introduce an Element into a Room

• Wooden furniture such as tables, chairs or stools. Wood can also be incorporated into furniture designs and panelling, or can be used for shutters or blinds made of bamboo or wooden slats. Wood is also present in raffia and chipboard, although the wood element is most powerful in solid wood itself.

• Ornaments such as letter or paper racks, jewellery or storage boxes, wooden sculptures, wooden bowls and dishes, vases or picture frames.

• Plants are a strong source of wood, particularly if they have woody stems. Bonsai trees, potted plants, fresh or dry flower arrangements can all be used.

• Fire and heat are natural sources of this element. A 'real' fire is the most powerful source, but fire is also strong in gas and electric fires or heaters.

• Light is also a source of fire, whether it is a table lamp or ceiling light, and if there is a fan attached to the light the fire element is further strengthened and circulated.

• Paintings, drawings or photographs that depict fire, heat or sunshine can all be used, as well as sculptures or ornaments that symbolize fire or heat.

• Earth itself in ceramic pots increases this element, as do yellow flowers, but be careful not to use woody-stemmed plants, since wood destroys earth in the destructive elemental cycle.

• Plain clay vases, plant pots or ornaments are also sources of the earth element, as are ceramic vases, bowls, tiles and china.

• Earth can also be depicted in paintings or drawings, but be aware that other elements may also be present in images, such as water or wood.

• Metal itself can be used in furniture or fittings as well as in ornaments. Metal vases, sculptures, candlesticks, cutlery, tools or picture frames will all strengthen the element. If you do use metal candlesticks, remember that fire is introduced if you light the candle.

• Clocks with a swinging pendulum are a useful source of metal, since they not only introduce the element but also increase its effectiveness through regular constant movement.

• Water in a clear vase is a strong source for this element, but do not allow the water to become dirty or stagnant. Clear glass is particularly good for holding water since it resembles ice, which is also a source of water energy. Water is strengthened with fountains or aquariums, since the movement of the water increases its energy.

• Water can be depicted in drawings or paintings, but avoid stormy scenes such as hurricanes or scenes of stagnant water, since both are powerfully yin.

The Pa Tzu Compass

The Pa Tzu compass is the guide to discovering your personal element. There are nine directions on the Pa Tzu compass, including the centre, and each one corresponds to a number, trigram, element and category known as Eastern or Western life, represented here by the letters E and W (see right). This compass follows the traditional Chinese south–north orientation.

How to Find Your Pa Tzu Number

The number that belongs to you depends upon the year of your birth. Once you have found your number (work through the calculations below), you can find out which element and trigram is associated with your character. This number is also the key to your personal compass, which follows a north–south orientation.

Now that you know your number you can find your Pa Tzu compass. The eight 'mini' compasses, which arise from the main Pa Tzu compass shown to the right, are divided into two groups called Eastern Life and Western Life. If your number is 1, 3, 4 or 9 you belong to the Eastern Life group, and your lucky directions are east, south-east, north and south. If your number

is 2, 6, 7 or 8 you belong to the Western Life group, and your lucky directions are west, south-west, north-west and north-east. If your number is 5 you should use compass 2 if you are male and compass 8 if you are female, as 5 represents the centre and does not have its own compass.

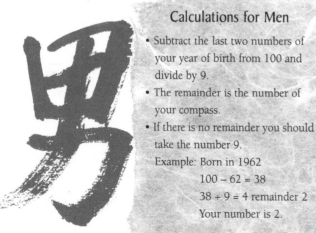

Calculations for Men

- Subtract the last two numbers of your year of birth from 100 and divide by 9.
- The remainder is the number of your compass.
- If there is no remainder you should take the number 9.

Example: Born in 1962

$$100 - 62 = 38$$
$$38 \div 9 = 4 \text{ remainder } 2$$

Your number is 2.

Calculations for Women

- Subtract 4 from the last two numbers of your year of birth and divide by 9.
- The remainder is the number of your compass.
- If there is no remainder you should take the number 9.

Example: Born in 1962

$$62 - 4 = 58$$
$$58 \div 9 = 6 \text{ remainder } 4$$

Your number is 4.

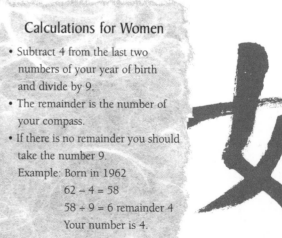

man

woman

Compass Categories

Each of the eight Pa Tzu compasses has four positive and four negative directions that cover different aspects of your fortune. On the traditional Pa Tzu compass the unlucky directions are called Five Ghosts, Death, Disaster and Unlucky Influences, but since these categories are not, in reality, as foreboding as they sound, they are represented here by the names Loss, Illness, Disagreement and Indecision respectively, which are more appropriate to their meanings.

The unlucky categories represent the possibility of negative fortune, but the weakness that lies in these areas can be corrected by introducing one or more of the five elements, as appropriate. Essentially, the categories simply mark the division of good and bad fortune, but they can also be linked to the aspects of life listed to the right:

- **Life** covers prosperity in relation to your family and career.
- **Good Fortune** relates to success in ideas, projects and contacts.
- **Vitality** relates to energy and general well-being.
- **Longevity** is linked to health and long life.
- **Loss** relates to the loss of objects, projects or finance.
- **Illness** covers lack of energy, tiredness as well as general ailments.
- **Disagreement** relates to setbacks and unexpected events.
- **Indecision** covers disappointments, delays and unforeseen difficulties.

Pa Tzu Compasses: Eastern Life

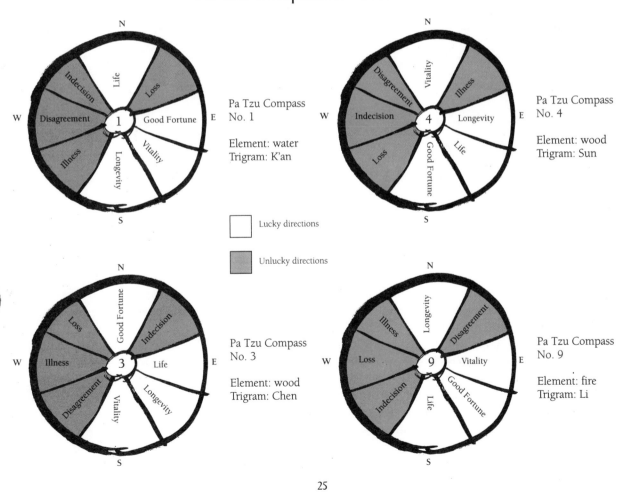

Pa Tzu Compass No. 1

Element: water
Trigram: K'an

Pa Tzu Compass No. 4

Element: wood
Trigram: Sun

Lucky directions

Unlucky directions

Pa Tzu Compass No. 3

Element: wood
Trigram: Chen

Pa Tzu Compass No. 9

Element: fire
Trigram: Li

Pa Tzu Compasses: Western Life

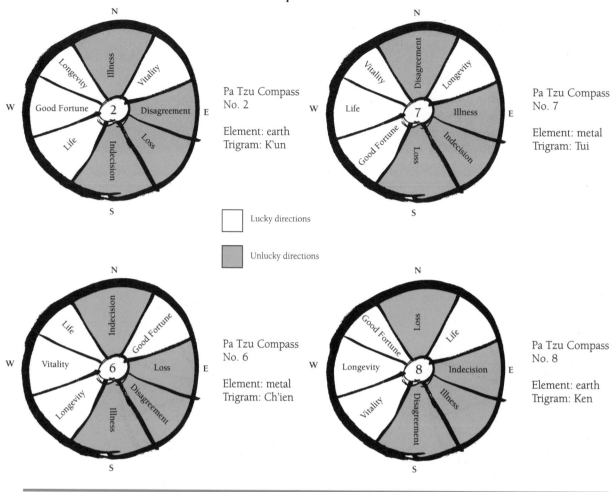

Pa Tzu Compass
No. 2

Element: earth
Trigram: K'un

Pa Tzu Compass
No. 7

Element: metal
Trigram: Tui

Lucky directions

Unlucky directions

Pa Tzu Compass
No. 6

Element: metal
Trigram: Ch'ien

Pa Tzu Compass
No. 8

Element: earth
Trigram: Ken

Using Your Compass

In Part Two you will find general feng shui guidelines for particular areas in and around your home and workplace, but in addition to following these guidelines you can also analyse the floor plan of your home or the layout of specific rooms to discover how they relate to your own year of birth. This is when you refer to your personal Pa Tzu compass. In order to take a reading all you need to know are your element and your lucky and unlucky directions (simply follow the calculations on page 24).

Each direction is associated with one of the five elements, and these always remain the same (*see top of page 27*). As we have already seen, some elements combine positively while others combine negatively. By using your Pa Tzu compass to take a reading you can find out which areas of your home or workplace need improving by checking how the element of the direction you are assessing combines with the element of your Pa Tzu compass.

The easiest way to use your compass is to draw a basic floor plan of the area or room you want

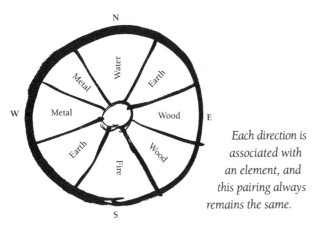

Each direction is associated with an element, and this pairing always remains the same.

you could stand in the centre of the area or room and use the compass printed in this book, pointing north on your Pa Tzu compass towards the northerly direction of the room.

If the room is an irregular shape some segments of the compass will not be fully covered. Do not try to adjust the reading by moving your position or by moving the compass; just work within the space allocated to each direction.

to assess (drawing it as accurately to scale as possible), and then draw your compass on top. You might find it helpful to draw your compass on a piece of tracing paper, so that you can simply overlay it on your floor plan, rather than drawing a new compass every time you wish to take a reading. The important thing to remember is that you must always align the north point of your compass with the northerly direction of the area you are assessing. Alternatively,

Shared Accommodation

If you live alone you only need to use your personal compass; if you are part of a family you should use the compass belonging to the main breadwinner. Each family member will, however, be able to carry out a reading for their bedroom or study. If you rent a house and there are several people living there, then focus your reading on your bedroom or apartment. The Pa Tzu compass helps to give you a more personalized reading, but there are also many general feng shui principles illustrated in the following sections that can help you understand the practice of feng shui.

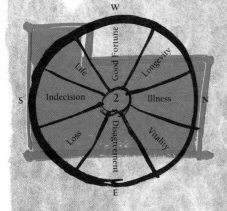

By overlaying your Pa Tzu compass on a floor plan you can discover where the weaknesses lie and which elements need to be strengthened or diminished.

Example

In the illustration to the left, Pa Tzu compass number 2 has been overlaid on a floor plan of a room. This compass belongs to the Western Life group, which means that the unlucky directions are north, east, south-east and south. These are the directions where the weaknesses lie, so you need to check how your Pa Tzu element (in this case, earth) combines with the elements of these directions (water, wood, wood and fire respectively). The elemental cycles show that earth destroys water, wood destroys earth and fire produces earth, so therefore the directions that require the most attention in this example are the east and south-east.

It is important that your Pa Tzu element is not overwhelmed in the negative areas, so you need to strengthen or diminish the elements as appropriate, using the advice on pages 22–3.

Feng Shui Solutions: Protecting a Site

There are several subtle but effective ways of dealing with negative energy travelling towards your home, of counteracting the effect of slow-moving ch'i or of energizing an area where ch'i is blocked. Sometimes the feng shui of a room can be improved simply by altering the arrangement of your furniture, by introducing greenery or by improving the lighting conditions. In other instances, architectural or natural features may be channelling destructive energy into your home and you may need to make use of a range of tools such as mirrors, blinds, screens, greenery, colours and light, all of which can be employed to offer protection and add balance.

The way you deal with negative energy depends on the force you are trying to counteract. Destructive energy can be blocked with blinds or screens, reflected with mirrors, absorbed by soft material, or bounced back with springs. This section guides you through a range of tools and how they can be used to protect a site and enhance ch'i in a particular area.

Mirrors

Traditionally, mirrors have been one of the most popular and effective feng shui tools. They continue to be widely used as a way to deflect malign forces and negative energy directed at a building or particular features. They are especially effective in reflecting back harmful energy channelled down knife-like roads or carried like an arrow from power lines or the pointed corner of a building. They also deflect the potentially detrimental effects from oncoming traffic, harmful reflections, sharp corners of natural features or roads, and the angular points of architectural features.

Any reflective surface – even a polished wok or tin foil – can be used instead of a mirror to achieve the desired effect.

Mirrors should be hung in line with the force approaching the building and should reflect the attacking object. For example, if you are protecting yourself from the powerful onrush of ch'i travelling down a straight road, the mirror should be large enough for the road to be reflected on its surface. The branch of a dead tree or the eaves of a roof pointing at a bedroom window might only need a small ornamental mirror.

Mirrors are also effective in activating slow-moving ch'i or energizing areas where ch'i may be blocked, since they reflect light and increase the feeling of space. For example, a mirror in a long narrow corridor will reflect back and enhance the energy of this area, or a mirror at the foot of basement stairs will help to bring yang into a yin area. When you are positioning mirrors, take care that part of your head is not cut off in the reflection; this is particularly relevant when the mirror is placed near the top or bottom of a staircase.

While mirrors are strong reflectors and enhancers, their effect can be overwhelming or startling if they are hung

28

either opposite each other, directly in the line of open doors or large windows or at the foot of the bed. Ch'i coming in through a door or window needs a chance to circulate and should not be immediately reflected back, while a mirror at the foot of a bed can give you an unexpected shock if you wake up suddenly.

Pa Kua Mirrors

The traditional feng shui mirror is called a *pa kua* mirror, and these can be bought at most Chinese supermarkets. They are small round mirrors set in a red wooden frame (in China, the colour red is associated with good fortune and prosperity). Below the mirror there is often a colourful painting of the god of the north (*see right*) or the fearsome god of war, both of whom are believed to ward off unlucky spirits. Around the mirror itself are the eight trigrams of the I Ching in the positions of the eight directions (*see page 14 for the interpretation of the trigrams*). The order of the trigrams follows the Former Heaven sequence – the earlier, alternative sequence to the trigrams that appear in the Pa Tzu system (the Pa Tzu compass follows the Later Heaven sequence). When reading these trigrams, the top line of the trigram is on the outside and the lower line on the inside.

Pa kua mirrors are usually hung above the front door of houses, restaurants or offices, but they can also be hung inside buildings. Although this traditional-style mirror is a popular feng shui tool you can use any mirror or reflective surface such as a pan, wok, polished piece of metal, tin foil, bowl or pool of water.

ABOVE *Powerful gods, such as the god of the north shown here, are traditionally depicted underneath pa kua mirrors to help deflect malign spirits.*

LEFT *Mirrors help to energize areas where ch'i may be sluggish or slow-moving, as they increase the feeling of space and light.*

Vegetation

Vegetation is an indication of healthy ch'i in and above the ground. It can have energizing and calming effects as well as being a useful means of strengthening and protecting a site. If one of the four animal spirits is weak around a building, trees or bushes can give additional support, or if your house is in a flat, featureless area, vegetation will help to prevent the dispersal of ch'i and accumulation of sha. Trees and bushes also act as screens to shield a building from fast-flowing ch'i on steep slopes or protect it from swift-moving traffic or the pressure created by corners of walls or other buildings.

Flowers and plants also play their role in activating ch'i on small balconies, patios and in the home or office. However, if you are introducing plants or flowers into a room, change the water regularly to prevent it becoming stagnant, keep the soil watered and remove the flowers or leaves if they begin to wilt. The same rule applies to the vegetation outside your home – a healthy green tree produces positive energy but a dead tree can be a source of negative energy.

If you are using vegetation to balance, protect and shield an area, do not overcrowd the space or plant so that the roots undermine the building. While trees are an indication of nourishing ch'i, if they overwhelm a house, blocking out the light and preventing the growth of other vegetation, they have an oppressive effect. You should also avoid random planting, since one well-sited tree can be more effective than a row of trees and bushes clumped together; evergreen trees are especially useful for single planting since they keep their cover.

Trees and plants can be used to activate ch'i, strengthen and protect a site, or screen against negative effects. They should not be overwhelming, however, and must always be kept healthy.

Colours

There are no absolute rules as to how or where colours should be used, although the guidelines in the section on the five elements (*see pages 22–3*) will help you to create a balance and use colour to strengthen your personal element. There may, however, be colours that make you feel uneasy, while others create a relaxing atmosphere, so you should also follow your personal preference.

A balanced use of colour enhances the feng shui of a room and creates a sense of harmony, whereas the excessive use of one colour can create an uneasy atmosphere. For example, an all-red room introduces a powerful fire element and may eventually make the occupants tense and argumentative. Since white is traditionally linked to mourning, an all-white room is considered unlucky and is also closely associated with hospitals and clinics.

If you want to use one colour as the main theme for a room, introduce other colours through textures, fabrics or ornaments so that one element does not dominate the room.

Blinds, Curtains and Porches

If you need to protect your home or office from roads or the cutting effect of corners, or from traffic travelling close by, you can create a barrier with blinds or curtains. The effect shields your house from negative or oppressive energy and gives you a layer of protection. If the front door is subject to destructive forces a porch can also serve this purpose, particularly if the entrance is moved to the side, away from the direct line of the front door.

Blinds and curtains are also used to prevent a disproportionate amount of ch'i entering a room. This principle applies for floor-to-ceiling single-pane windows or for windows that run the full length of the room, since their size and position may allow excessive sunlight or cold to enter the room.

Pictures and Symbols

Paintings, photographs and drawings can all be used to create an atmosphere of activity, liveliness or relaxation. Fertile landscapes are particularly useful since they depict nourishing energy, whereas a scarred or stunted landscape indicates an absence of life-giving ch'i. A picture can also be used to strengthen an element when you are using the Pa Tzu system. For example, a waterfall or river will increase the water element, or a painting of a red sunset or burning leaves will improve the fire element. Images linked with violence, decay or death depict destructive forces, so avoid hanging them in your home, where the emphasis should be on harmony and balance.

Sculptures, Textures and Household Objects

Depending on the nature of the force you have to combat, sculptures, textures and household objects can all be effective tools. For example, if the branches of a dead tree are pointing towards your house you could place the blade of a saw outside your home, since it has a cutting effect on the attacking force. If you use a real saw, take care to ensure that it is placed well out of children's reach; alternatively, a safer option is simply to use a model of a saw, or to file

Blinds (above) *can be used as a barrier, while paintings* (below) *can invoke an atmosphere or strengthen an element. Springs* (below left) *can bounce away negative energy.*

Many Chinese homes or businesses have a fish tank or aquarium, since fish are thought to denote good fortune and healthy finance – the Chinese word for 'fish' (yu) sounds similar to that for excess (yu).

down the sharp teeth. The powerful energy of television or satellite aerials can be absorbed by materials such as sand, foam or wood chips placed in an open basket, box or tray. Springs positioned on the roof or outside your home or office help to ward off the effect of overpowering buildings or angular structures by bouncing back their incoming force. In these examples the tools you use should be placed in line with the attacking object in order for them to be effective.

When you are thinking of ways to protect part of a building from a negative force, take time to study the nature of the force. If you are trying to counteract the effect of sharp architectural features, telephone wires, electric cables or aerials you can soften and absorb their impact on your home. The effect of taller buildings, sharp corners or roads directed at your home can also be bounced off so that the force is broken up into a variety of directions. If you are protecting your house or apartment from shapes that resemble weapons or animals ready to attack, either in the landscape or on buildings, you can protect the site by using pointed or cutting objects. (Models or sculptures should be used to avoid accidents.)

Water

Water has strong life-giving qualities that encourage and nourish the flow of ch'i, but if it is low-lying or stagnant it then becomes a source of sha – malign energy. Fresh flowers in a glass vase can enliven the flow of sluggish or blocked ch'i in a room, while a fountain in a lobby or foyer attracts beneficial ch'i into the building. A fish pond or ornamental pool in a front garden is also said to attract good fortune from distant places. The gentle movement of water is life-giving and yang – this is seen in the flow of a river or the smooth swell of the sea – but when water is hit by violent storms or becomes stagnant it has strong yin qualities and can be destructive. This same principle applies to ponds, pools and aquariums. Healthy plant life that improves the aeration of the water, or fish moving through the water, enliven ch'i and have yang qualities.

Curves and Symmetry

Circles and round structures are a sign of something that is complete as well as being an indication of satisfaction and happiness. Round structures or architectural features enable ch'i to flow evenly and smoothly, whereas sharp features can pierce ch'i and cluttered spaces break its flow.

If you are designing a garden, buying a house or choosing furniture, aim for curves and balance so that an overall symmetry is created. While it is not always possible to find accommodation with domed roofs, features such as curved pathways, window frames, porches or arches all enhance the flow of energy around the site. Complete shapes also provide more positive readings than irregular designs. For example, a rectangular or square plot of land is preferable to one that has sides of different lengths, while a room with two bays is more balanced than one with one narrow extension. Sometimes a structure can accommodate unusual shapes or uneven sections if it creates an overall impression of balance and proportion and relates harmoniously to the landforms around it.

Rounded, symmetrical furniture encourages a smooth flow of ch'i around a room.

Wind Chimes

Wind chimes were traditionally used in China to frighten away unsettled spirits or 'Hungry Ghosts'. These are believed to be the spirits of the deceased who have been buried without adequate funeral rites and continue to wander the earth. At New Year they are frightened off with firecrackers but at the Hungry Ghost festival, on the fifteenth day of the seventh lunar month, their spirits are appeased with offerings, prayers and liturgies in the hope that they will be placated and respond benevolently.

Wind chimes have now gained a wider usage and are hung to help dispel negative forces as well as activate ch'i in an area where it may be slow-moving. They are also a useful indicator of someone entering a room in situations where your view of the door is obstructed.

Wind chimes activate slow-moving ch'i and dispel negative forces.

harmony

Improving Your Feng Shui

This part of the workbook takes you on a step-by-step journey through the rural landscape and into an urban environment, including readings for specific rooms in your home or workplace. The general principles and guidelines contained in each section are intended to help you understand the flow of ch'i in specific areas and determine why it may be disturbed or blocked. Suggestions to improve weak areas or encourage a more even circulation of ch'i are offered throughout.

How to Use Part Two

flow

In this part of the book, a wide range of examples are covered, from the pattern of roads around your home to the design of your house or apartment. We have looked at the most favourable positions for items of furniture, particularly sofas, cookers, beds and desks, and their siting in relation to doors and windows, and have, where applicable, suggested simple solutions. These are, however, guidelines and not absolute rules. Every home and every person is different, and you may feel very comfortable, relaxed and protected without having to make any alterations. For example, if you are studying at home or working in an office, your back should have the support of a wall to help you concentrate, but you may find that sitting at a desk facing an open window enables you to focus on your work and increases your productivity. Perhaps you find the amount of light entering helpful, or the view inspirational – therefore you should follow your judgement.

On other occasions you may feel something needs changing but are not sure where or how to begin. Our guidelines will help you understand how the shape or position of structures or furniture might exert an oppressive influence, or how open doors and windows may make you feel vulnerable or drained. Sometimes a minor alteration to your surroundings, such as clearing away clutter, hanging a blind or introducing gentle lighting, can exert a subtle and positive change. The guidelines are there to help you, not disturb you, and you should follow what you feel is most appropriate to your circumstances.

Each section in this part of the book is highly visual, and the 'at-a-glance' illustrations allow you to understand immediately whether the feng shui in each example is good or 'bad'. The unique key system reinforces this instant interpretation: every illustration features a symbol that identifies whether the feng shui depicted is good, 'bad' or whether steps have been taken to remedy the situation, and thus the feng shui is 'improved' (*see above right*). You should refer to all the illustrations in order to determine which aspects of the examples shown are most applicable to your own surroundings.

Advice is given for all situations where the feng shui needs improving, so helpful suggestions will always be at your fingertips (please note that in

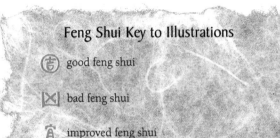

Feng Shui Key to Illustrations

(good feng shui symbol) good feng shui

(bad feng shui symbol) bad feng shui

(improved feng shui symbol) improved feng shui

some instances the same advice applies to two or more illustrations). Once you become familiar with the principles, you will begin to get a feel for an 'ideal' feng shui site and apply this knowledge to your own surroundings.

The Landscape

Feng shui literally means 'wind/water' and you can see the powerful shaping effects of these forces in the natural world. A cold, windswept site often has low, patchy vegetation so ch'i is quickly dispersed, whereas a landscape of gentle hills and rivers allows for greater plant growth and provides protection from the elements. In the rural section, a variety of landforms and river courses are illustrated, and the type of energy they create is also explored. On a wider level there is the overall balance created by the hills, plains or rivers, but there are also animal and elemental shapes and patterns in the land or on water, all of which have an effect on those living nearby.

Roads, Homes and Offices

Many of the principles that apply to the flow of rivers also apply to the pattern of roads; similarly, the principles for a well-protected rural site also apply to an urban site. The range of examples given can be used whether you live in a small town or in the heart of a city. A variety of housing styles are covered, ranging from high-rise apartment blocks to detached houses. While different types of home share many of the same guidelines, specific needs of the varying styles are also discussed.

The demands of the workplace are different to domestic needs, and so the business section stands on its own. Since businesses are usually reliant on clients or customers, they should be sited in busy areas where there is already flourishing business ch'i. They are also able to thrive on a greater degree of activity, traffic and noise than would suit a normal household. You should, however, gauge the information according to the nature of your work. If your work is dependent upon a quiet environment, you may find that the section on the shape of buildings and layout of offices is more pertinent than the section on the site of a business.

Taking a Pa Tzu Reading

As discussed on page 27, you can take a personal Pa Tzu reading for a complete floor plan of your home or office, or for a specific room. The kitchen, living room and main bedroom are traditionally the most important domestic rooms and so sample readings have been included for each of these rooms. You can, however, choose to carry out a reading for any room in your home, but remember to align north on your Pa Tzu compass with the northern direction of the room. In the workplace, the position of desks is important inside an office, particularly the manager's or director's desk, and so a sample reading is given for a small open-plan office.

Where relevant in the sample readings, suggestions for change are offered according to the elemental combinations. These are not, however, hard and fast rules, and if you feel the room already has a positive and smooth flow of ch'i then changes may not be necessary.

Outside the Home

Ch'i is manifest in all natural phenomena: it is seen in towering peaks, steep cliffs, fertile land, rolling hills, open plains or fast-flowing rivers. In each place ch'i is different, sometimes dangerous, other times benevolent. For example, a site where stormy waters break against craggy cliffs is powerfully yin and the ch'i here can be overwhelming, but water spreading gently across fertile land is yang and the ch'i is life-giving. The ideal site combines even-flowing, active ch'i, both on land and in water, to create a balance between yin and yang; when the two are in harmony they nourish and energize each other.

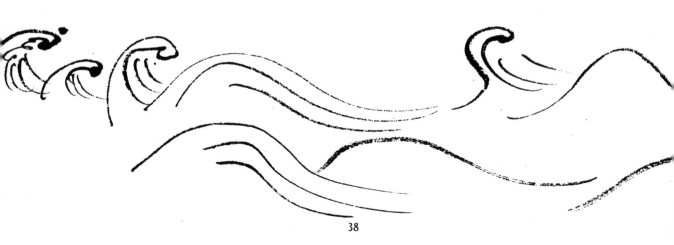

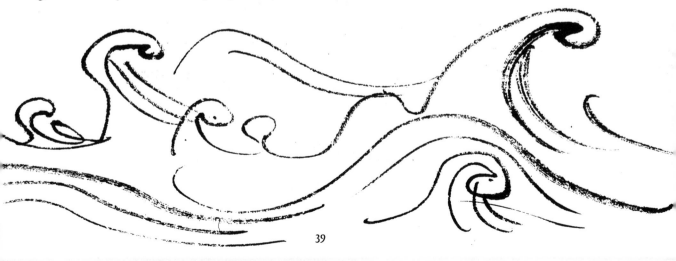

In this section we look at the energy that is present in and around landforms and the influence it may have on that site. Examples are given of specific patterns and shapes that can be identified in the land, on water and in roads (in both rural and urban situations), since the 'flow' of roads follows many of the principles that apply to the flow of watercourses. There are, of course, hundreds of forms that can be read in the landscape by an experienced feng shui practitioner, but this brief section opens the way to seeing and understanding the landscape from a new perspective.

Mountains, Hills and Rivers

While ch'i is present in all places to a greater or lesser extent, the actual shapes of the land, rivers and sites where the land meets the sea are identified with elements, animals, birds and other phenomena. Some are seen as guardians protecting the site, making it a safe and auspicious place, while others are ready to devour the site, bringing misfortune to those who live there. Some are passive and do not convey any particular influence on an area, and others are dynamic, producing powerful and effective energy.

This section shows you how to interpret these various shapes in the landscape and determine whether they have a positive or negative effect on your surroundings.

The Four Guardians

In feng shui, the classic guardians of a site are the Green Dragon, Red Bird, Black Tortoise and White Tiger, as we discovered earlier on page 18. These are the creatures that can be identified in the actual lie of the land around any site. They may be perfectly proportioned, bringing good fortune to the area, but sometimes the landforms associated with them are weak and, therefore, their protective power is diminished. When these four creatures are in harmony with one another, the site benefits from smooth and beneficial ch'i.

An ideal site for the animal spirits: they are balanced in the landscape, protecting the house in the centre.

Animal Forms in the Land

Specific features in the land can bestow an energetic quality on the landscape. Sometimes a site has the basic shape of an animal but it is not as powerful as a site that depicts the animal when it is in motion.

For example, when the shape of a Swan or a Snake appears in the landscape it offers a positive reading (*see illustrations opposite*). The land will prove to be a good site on which a family can live for a generation, but it will not be able to sustain continual building by successive generations. When the animal is in motion, however, such as the Swan diving into water or the Snake leaving a mountain, the land is endowed with regenerative qualities that can sustain a

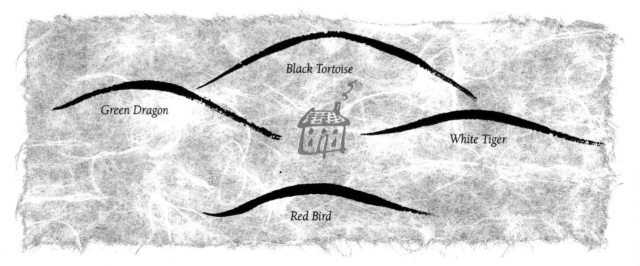

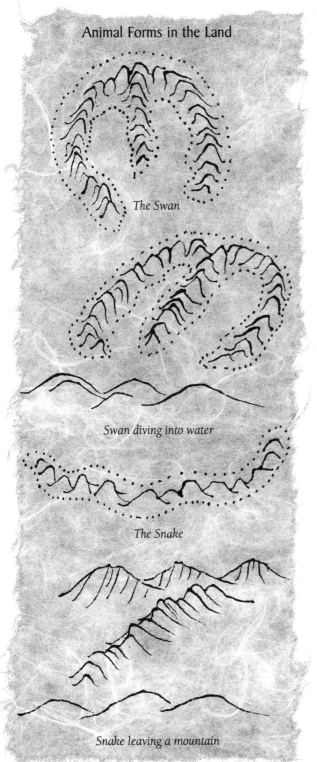

Animal Forms in the Land

The Swan

Swan diving into water

The Snake

Snake leaving a mountain

variety of use. In addition to producing beneficial chi, these active landforms also have the power to store and spread ch'i.

There is a wide variety of intricate animal formations that will be familiar to a skilled feng shui practitioner; however, it is still possible for any one of us to look carefully at the land and read its shapes. Certain formations take on a nourishing aspect: the hills may form wide, gently sweeping arms and the sites may nestle inside, resembling a dragon protecting a pearl. Other sites may have a more ominous energy – for example, the shape of jagged cliffs might look like tigers ready to pounce. The important rule is to stop and study the site, look at its shapes and forms, follow the basic guidelines and see what sort of energy emanates from the area.

The Water Dragon

Just as animals can be seen in the contours of the land, they can also be identified in the contours of a river and the surface patterns created by the flow of water. While specific animals might be associated with certain shapes, the actual twists, branches and bends of all rivers are known as the Water Dragon. The many formations that watercourses follow are given a feng shui interpretation in a Chinese text known as the Water Dragon Classic. Here the ideal site nestles within the inner curves of a watercourse that is nourished by an outer, curved watercourse, thereby protecting the site in the 'stomach of the dragon'. Gently flowing water that follows a meandering course also creates nourishing ch'i, and sites located in these curves are 'embraced' by the Water Dragon.

If the flow of water is hurried and turbulent the site is drained of energy, while straight or sharply turning rivercourses are like 'secret arrows' cutting into the wealth and health of those living nearby. Such unfavourable sites need protection in the form of other buildings or natural features – raised land or vegetation, for instance. Examples of various sites are shown overleaf.

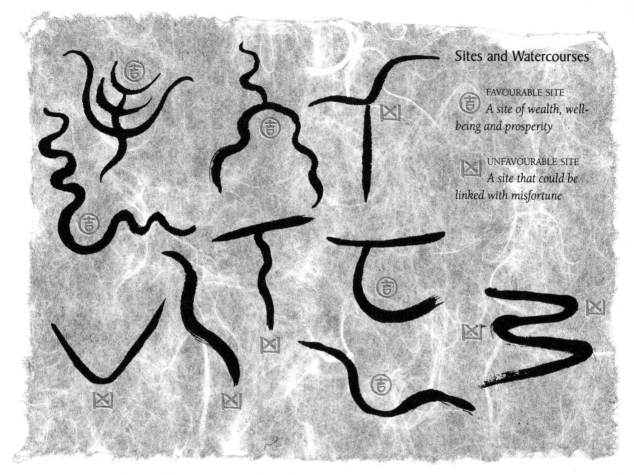

Sites and Watercourses

FAVOURABLE SITE
A site of wealth, well-being and prosperity

UNFAVOURABLE SITE
A site that could be linked with misfortune

Coastal Waters and Lakes

Readings for coastal waters are taken from the patterns created by the wind, by its contact with the land and by the channels of water that flow into the sea. Readings for lakes are also judged by the surface patterns as well as by the shape of the lake and the tributaries leading to it.

As with the land formations, there is an extensive set of patterns that can be identified in a body of water by an experienced feng shui practitioner. For the less experienced, the key to understanding water formations is to look for water with an even flow or a regular pattern so that the ch'i created not only nourishes the land but also enriches those living in the vicinity. Sluggish, stagnant or polluted water is a source of sha (destructive vapours), while rapid-flowing or rough water can quickly disperse ch'i.

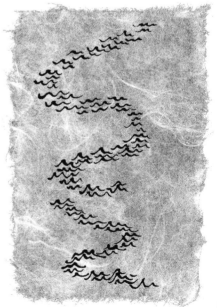

The pattern created by the wind on the surface of this water creates an animated and auspicious shape called 'Submerged Dragon Swirls Tail'.

The Five Elements

The five elements of wood, fire, earth, metal and water can be seen in specific shapes in the land, rivers and streams. Sometimes the elements are repeated in a certain sequence or they combine to produce sites that possess powerful and productive ch'i (*see examples below*). Once you are familiar with the relationship between the elements, you should be able to identify the elemental shapes in the landscape and determine whether they are harmonious or whether the patterns they form are negative.

Land

Many land formations are traditionally used as examples of identifying combinations of elements in the land – some have even been attributed with symbolic names. For example, the

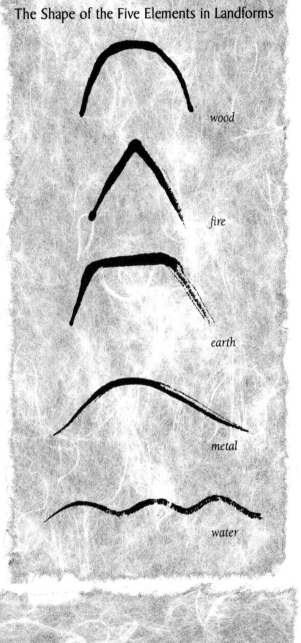

The Shape of the Five Elements in Landforms

wood

fire

earth

metal

water

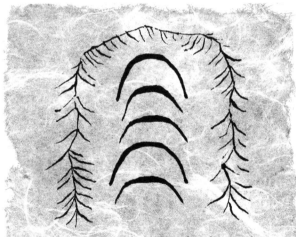

Series of wood-shaped peaks

A fortunate combination of elements known as 'Roots Digging Deep into Firm Foundations'.

water   *wood*   *earth*

sequence of wood-shaped peaks shown on page 43 forms a series of 'ascending steps'. It is also surrounded and protected by a mountain range. This formation is productive and fortunate since the pattern of the peaks is likened to a ladder ascending to the sky.

In the landscape illustrated at the bottom of page 43, the range of hills shaped like the water element nourishes the wood-shaped hill, and together they meet earth, which gives them a solid grounding. This produces a range of mountains known as 'Roots Digging Deep into Firm Foundations'. The formation of this site is said to grant prosperity and wealth.

Water

According to the Water Dragon Classic, the elements of water, earth and metal are the luckiest combinations since their shapes are softer and more gentle, thereby encouraging the even and productive flow of ch'i.

When different river shapes combine they can create beneficial or unlucky feng shui, depending once again on whether these elements have a creative or destructive relationship. For example, a water-shaped river entering a metal-shaped river is a positive combination and a site here is likely to receive its beneficial influence, whereas a fire-shaped river entering a metal-shaped river could exert a malign influence on the site, since fire destroys metal.

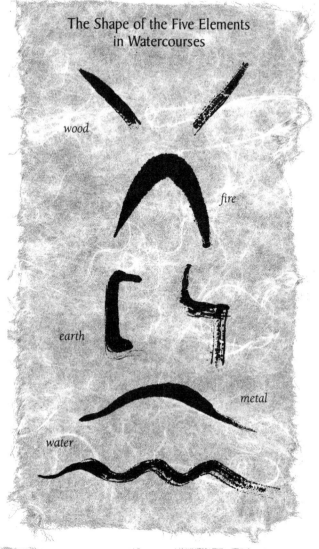

The Shape of the Five Elements in Watercourses

wood

fire

earth

metal

water

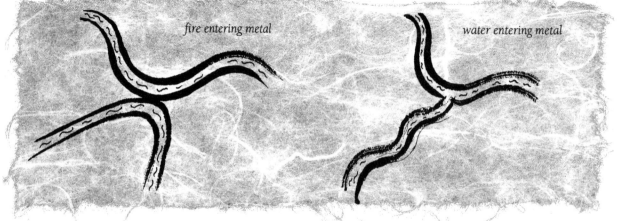

fire entering metal

water entering metal

Feng Shui in Rural Landscapes

If you live in a rural landscape you are very close to the deep energy that exists in landforms and can include local and distant features in your reading. One of the most important factors to consider is the level of protection offered by the natural environment. Ideally, the four guardians should be seen in raised land behind and on either side of your house. The land should not be scarred or devoid of vegetation, as this saps the earth's energy. The height, shape and proportion of raised features also need to be observed, since these can overshadow your home or create narrow wind-tunnels or a downward rush of ch'i.

Houses that are isolated and open to the elements are also vulnerable. In the absence of natural protective features, build a screen of trees or erect other buildings to act as a defence against adverse weather and the uncontrolled flow of ch'i.

A classic example of a well-sited house is one situated on a gentle slope, protected behind by raised land and facing out towards a bay so that land and water meet harmoniously. Traditionally in feng shui, an ideal site would be south-facing to benefit from the light and warmth of the sun.

A house perched on the top of a hill or cliff is too isolated and ch'i is quickly dispersed. It is like a lonely guard on a hill and needs other buildings, fences or trees to provide protection.

good feng shui   bad feng shui   improved feng shui

If the hill behind the house is too steep the beneficial ch'i rolls straight past the house, and as a result the occupants may find that good fortune quickly slips away. These houses need support, both at the back and the front, in order to curb the fast flow of ch'i.

ABOVE *An overhanging cliff is oppressive for those living underneath, since its weight presses down like a lid. Pointed objects could be placed on the roof of the house to resemble chisels cutting into and weakening the weight of the rock.*

The front of the house should not be enclosed by clumps of trees, which have powerful yang energy and also prevent light from entering the house. The height and density of the trees should be kept under control and the occupant should be alert to the possibility of the trees' roots undermining the foundations of the building.

ABOVE *This house faces a cliff that resembles a tiger ready to pounce. Certain shapes in the land can bestow positive energy since they resemble auspicious features, such as a book or pen indicating scholarly success, but this crouched tiger is potentially dangerous. Instal a mirror to reflect the tiger's image and place a hunting weapon (or a replica of one, for safety considerations) in the direction of the rock.*

good feng shui bad feng shui improved feng shui

The hillside near this house has a smooth indent resembling a large rice bowl, which could be seen as a sign of a regular food supply and, therefore, prosperity. The land in front also gently rises, so the house is not overpowered by the gradient of the hill.

The current from electric pylons close to a row of houses could throw ch'i into disarray and affect the health and relationships of those living there. Their impact can be reflected back or absorbed by a large tray or box of absorbent material such as wood chips or sand.

These houses are set in a wide, gently undulating valley, protected by a higher range of hills to the back and slightly lower ones to the side and front, echoing the ideal four-guardian formation. A site such as this is conducive to an efficient and smooth flow of ch'i.

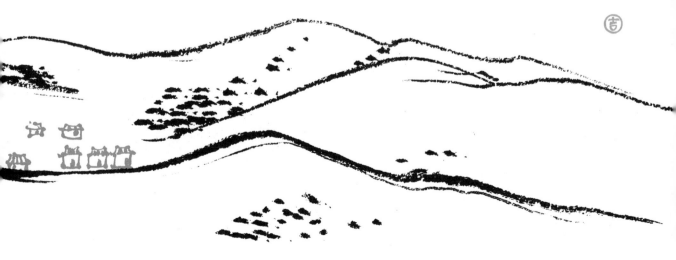

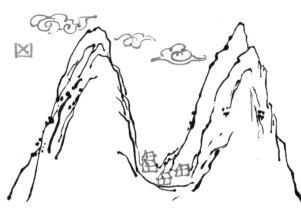

BELOW *The hills around these houses are dotted with shrubs and stunted bushes, giving the impression of scars or spots, which could affect the health of the nearby residents. Try to landscape the area around the houses with well-kept trees and flowers to produce life-giving ch'i and, if possible, incorporate round structures in your design.*

ABOVE *Ch'i is oppressed and trapped by the steep hills and narrow valley floor. The amount of light entering is limited, and the valley could act as a wind-tunnel funnelling ch'i and negative forces rapidly through this space. Although the landform cannot be altered, the occupants should try to shield the immediate area around their houses from this rapid flow. Trees or terracing on the hillside would also help to control ch'i running quickly down these slopes.*

ABOVE *This featureless landscape is dotted with low-lying sparse vegetation and is subject to strong winds, so ch'i passes swiftly and is soon dispersed. The house needs protection from outbuildings or trees to avoid it being the target for destructive energy.*

Although these houses are built on flat land with few raised features, the trees and shrubs help to regulate the flow of ch'i and enable it to circulate smoothly. Buildings such as gazebos or small barns would also help control energy flow.

Road Patterns

Roads are major channels along which ch'i circulates, and therefore they influence the energy in your home and local area. The flow of ch'i depends on the formation of the roads and their relationship with natural or man-made features. Roads are the urban equivalent of rivers in a rural landscape, so many of the rules that apply to watercourses also apply to roads.

The most beneficial ch'i is created by gently curved roads. Ch'i is concentrated at busy intersections or converging roads, is blocked in narrow, cramped conditions and is funnelled down straight arrow-like roads. The flow of ch'i can quickly change if it is confronted by a sudden narrowing of a wide road, when it meets a series of sharp bends, or when it is abruptly trapped by a dead-end and its negative effects rebound on the nearby buildings. The condition of road surfaces also affects feng shui. Surfaces should be even and well-maintained; smooth earth roads are the most beneficial, since they are directly in contact with the earth's energy.

The pattern and shape of roads also take on certain characteristics that influence the site. A gently curved road wraps itself around sites like a 'jade belt', a V-shaped road resembles scissors cutting into the site, a flyover can be likened to a scythe, while an even, winding road may resemble a dragon and thus bestow good fortune on that site.

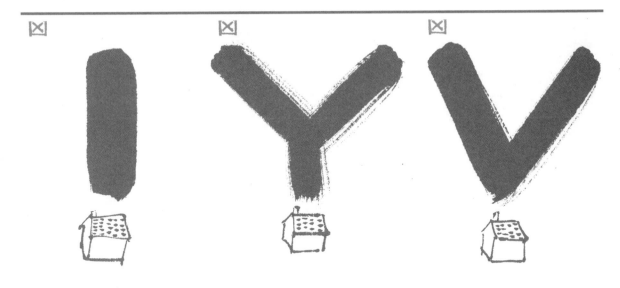

A house or apartment block built at the end of a long, straight road is subject to sha because of the force of the energy being funnelled down this direct, narrow route. (See advice on page 50.)

The Y-shaped road causes confusion for the occupants of this building. They may find it hard to make important family or business decisions. (See advice on page 50.)

Destructive forces are focused at the sharp point where the road forms a V. The negative energy that accumulates at this point could affect the health and relationships of those living nearby. (See advice on page 50.)

good feng shui   bad feng shui   improved feng shui

A house or apartment on one of the corners of a crossroads is subject to the convergence of ch'i from several directions and the sharp corners accentuate destructive ch'i. The house is also affected by the movement of traffic from four directions, particularly when vehicles turning at the crossroads appear to be heading towards the front door. A mirror outside the house will help to deflect the influence of oncoming traffic, while blinds offer added protection.

Houses built on the outside bend of roads or flyovers suffer from the 'scything' effect of the bend. This knife-like effect needs to be controlled. (See advice below.)

• **Advice** A mirror or other reflective object can be used to reflect back destructive energy; the mirror's energy will be enhanced if a small sword or spear (or a model of one) is placed above it, pointing towards the road. It will also help the site if there is a curved pathway leading to the building to control the flow of ch'i as well as ease the effect of negative forces. The front door could be screened with a porch, and a row of bushes or small trees will give added protection.

good feng shui   bad feng shui   improved feng shui

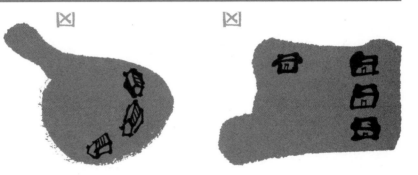

ABOVE *Since there is only one narrow exit from these culs-de-sac, the energy is easily trapped. The residents may find that their finances and general good fortune are being squeezed out; the circular site (left) even resembles a noose. Additional small exits or pathways would help to prevent energy becoming trapped and decayed.*

LEFT *The ch'i travelling down the road towards the T-junction becomes too forceful as it meets the intersections and can affect the prosperity of those facing the junction or living at a point between the two junctions. Use reflective objects to protect the site and create a barrier with blinds, shrubs or fencing.*

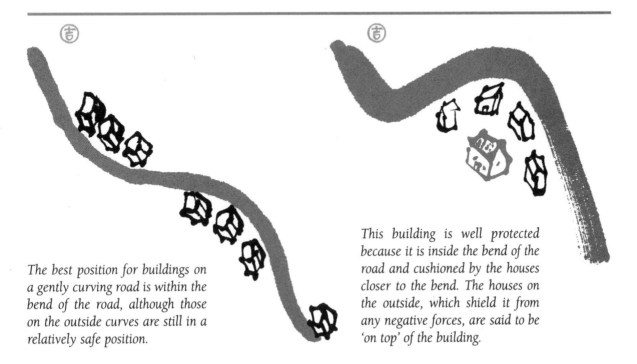

The best position for buildings on a gently curving road is within the bend of the road, although those on the outside curves are still in a relatively safe position.

This building is well protected because it is inside the bend of the road and cushioned by the houses closer to the bend. The houses on the outside, which shield it from any negative forces, are said to be 'on top' of the building.

A complex pattern of roads with many twists and corners can confuse and trap the flow of ch'i. Try to create positive conditions in and around your house or apartment using greenery, rounded structures or designs and appropriate light conditions.

Roads that converge near a bridge are a powerful meeting point for energy. While this busy site might be suitable for a shop or restaurant, it can be overwhelming for a domestic residence, which would need to be well shielded by trees or a fence. Blinds or curtains can be used as a barrier, and a mirror helps deflect forceful energy. The houses down the side-road are better protected.

When roads branch off a main circular road, the homes that nestle within the inner branches receive the most beneficial ch'i.

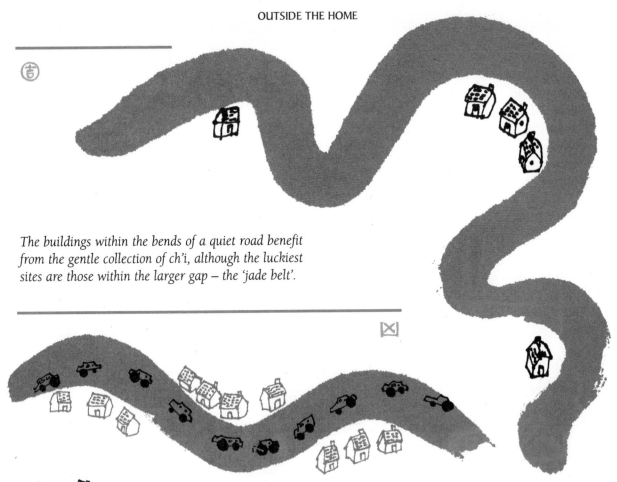

The buildings within the bends of a quiet road benefit from the gentle collection of ch'i, although the luckiest sites are those within the larger gap – the 'jade belt'.

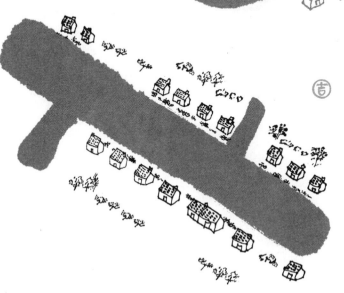

ABOVE LEFT *Although these houses are well-sited on this road, the good fortune normally associated with the site is reduced if there is a continual, heavy flow of traffic.*

LEFT *Many houses or apartment blocks are built along flat, straight roads, but this does not necessarily mean they have bad feng shui. The reading depends upon traffic flow, house structure, the amount of natural vegetation and the surrounding features. Assess these aspects before deciding whether countermeasures are needed.*

good feng shui   bad feng shui   improved feng shui

Features around the Home

When you are looking at a house or apartment there are many factors that you automatically take into consideration. One is likely to be its position in relation to other buildings – is it dwarfed by neighbouring buildings, making it look dark or squashed? Perhaps it towers over its neighbours, providing a wonderful view but also making it isolated and vulnerable to the elements? You may also judge it according to its decorative appearance or structural design, and notice that the colour of the bricks jars against the immediate environment, the window frames are rotting or the front door is out of proportion to the rest of the house. These are all factors that are considered when assessing the feng shui of a building.

There are, however, many other points to take into account. Although less obvious, they could have a detrimental or enriching effect on the circulation of ch'i. These include the shape of the plot of land, for example: are there many curved or straight lines in the paths, borders or features of the building, or are the sharp corners of other buildings or power lines pointing directly towards your home?

This section covers a wide variety of sites and conditions, working inwards from the position of your house or apartment block in relation to other buildings through to assessing the access to the front door – the main pathway of ch'i into your home.

Houses in Relation to Other Buildings

The site of your home needs to be protected by neighbouring features but also needs adequate space for energy to circulate. In built-up areas structures surrounding your home represent the four animal guardians; in a semi-urban area the guardians can be seen in trees, neighbouring houses and landforms. Assess the angles and size of nearby structures for sharp corners or other features 'cutting' into your fortune.

Do taller buildings overshadow your home, or electric pylons and cables point in your direction? Some sites, such as playgrounds, convey positive energy, while a waste disposal site can be negative. Be aware of changing patterns around you, such as reflections from other buildings, fumes or disruptive noise. You cannot usually change local features, but mirrors, vegetation or screens can afford protection.

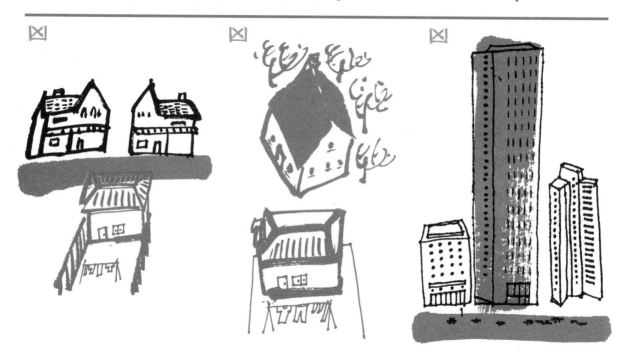

A house or apartment should not face a gap between two buildings, since the occupants' savings might slip through the narrow space. Move the main door so that it is not opposite the gap, or screen the door with a porch; in addition, the windows could be shielded with shutters or blinds.

If the corner of a building faces the front of a house, it acts like a knife cutting into the owner's prosperity. A mirror would reflect back negative forces, but you can also shield the house with a row of trees, a fence (preferably covered in greenery) or with blinds on the windows facing the corner.

Tall, thin buildings that tower over neighbouring buildings are isolated and open to the elements. Ch'i is quickly dispersed and the upper part of the building is open to destructive energy. Individual apartments can be protected with mirrors, blinds or curtains. Plants will also help to achieve ch'i.

ABOVE *Tall buildings overshadowing the front or back of this house prevent light entering and exert pressure on the smaller house.*

ABOVE RIGHT *The fortune of the middle house is squeezed by the weight of the taller houses.*

• **Advice** *Knife-shaped objects or metal springs on the roof of the smaller building will act as a defence against the overpowering effect of the taller buildings (beware of bouncing destructive energy directly into a neighbour's house). If possible, greenery and water on the roof will also help to enliven ch'i.*

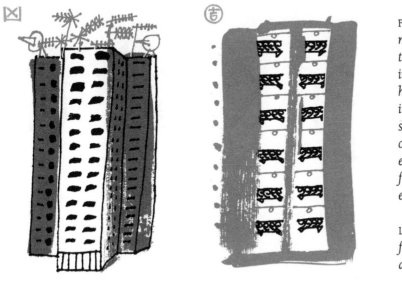

FAR LEFT *Aerials, satellites and masts are like weapons that cut through ch'i. Avoid living in or facing these buildings, but if you do not have a choice you can absorb their impact with soft materials such as sand or send it back with reflective objects. If you are using mirrors, ensure that aerials or masts are fully reflected, so their destructive energy is sent straight back.*

LEFT *Small balconies on a block of flats do not disturb the overall balance of the building.*

good feng shui   bad feng shui   improved feng shui

ABOVE *The houses alongside your house should be a similar height, those behind should be slightly higher to offer protection, while the land or features in front should be lower. This design conforms to the ideal positions for the four animal guardians surrounding a site.*

RIGHT *A large building behind your house or apartment not only prevents light entering but acts as an oppressive force. You need to reflect or bounce this force away. Alternatively you can cut into it with pointed triangular shapes on your roof.*

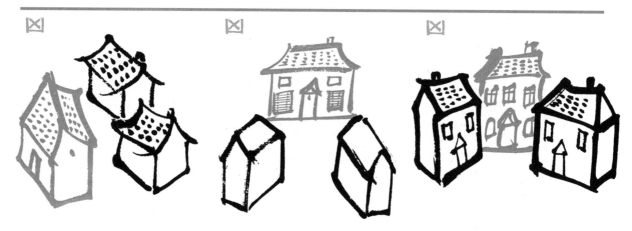

The roofs of houses located behind, to the side or in front of your house should not point towards your house as though they are piercing it. The pointed edges of sloping roofs in particular can cut into your home.

• **Advice** *The cutting effect of roofs can be controlled by softening their impact with a tree, or with greenery growing up the outside of your house. Blinds on the windows that are in line with the points of the roof facing your house will also have a shielding effect, as will a small mirror hanging on the wall or in the window affected.*

Even if your house is well-positioned in relation to other houses, be aware of power lines, sharp corners, pointed features and other subtle but negative forces that are directed at your home. The effect of satellites and aerials can be absorbed with sand or wood chips, or bounced back with springs. A pair of open scissors placed under power lines is also effective. Remove dead trees or vegetation close to your home, and try to create rounded edges to reduce the strength of negative forces and encourage a gentle flow of ch'i.

Many people do not mind overlooking a cemetery or a place associated with illness and death, but if you do feel uneasy or uncomfortable put blinds on the windows or hang wind chimes over the door because they are believed to frighten away wandering spirits.

Places where the community gathers for prayer and meditation, or healing centres, often generate positive ch'i into the area. The same principle applies for schools, playgrounds and day centres, as they are all places of activity, learning and care.

Plots of Land

The plots of land illustrated below can be used for readings on detached houses, small rows of houses, or apartment blocks. There are two main considerations: firstly, the balance created by the building in relation to the surrounding land and, secondly, the ability of ch'i to circulate freely.

Ch'i is most beneficial when it can flow smoothly over and around a site – thus curves and round edges create better conditions than sharp corners or straight lines. In a triangular plot, for example, destructive energy can settle within the sharp, angular corners. This can create unfavourable circumstances since the house is contained within these points. If the land itself cannot be rounded off, you can create shields to block this energy, introduce objects to reflect it or construct curved lines to enhance the flow of ch'i. A building also needs support and light – a lack of support at the back of the house can affect the stability and health of those living there, while lack of light limits the beneficial effect of ch'i as well as creates a feeling of oppression.

The best plots of land are those that are rectangular or square with a larger area at the back than at the front to provide protection in the Black Tortoise position. Ideally the land should slope gently from back to front, but if the gradient is too steep and there is nothing to protect the house ch'i quickly rolls away, draining the good fortune from the site.

There is an overall balance here between the house and the plot of land. The back garden is larger than the front garden, offering support, and the trees at the back add protection and round off the edges.

If there is a large, flat and featureless area at the back, give the house some support with features such as bushes, a rounded gazebo, small trees, or an ivy-covered fence.

good feng shui   bad feng shui   improved feng shui

If the back garden is small, do not overcrowd the space with trees, sheds or a garage. Blinds or curtains on the back windows, or mirrors above the door, can give protection from overpowering features.

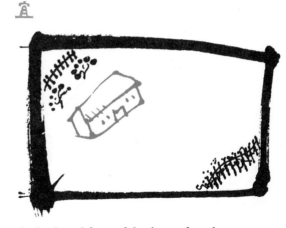

The back and front of this house face sharp corners, so round off the points with a screen – either an ivy-covered fence or bushes. You can also use mirrors to deflect any malign influences that might accumulate in these corners.

Although this garden is relatively long this is a positive layout, since the proportions are balanced. The house is given plenty of support at the back from the large garden, while the trees soften the edges and shield the house.

If there is a lack of space directly in front of the house, open land beyond the front garden will balance the site. If there is a road nearby, erect a small screen of bushes and curve the pathway leading to the front door to create the illusion of distance.

In a plot with sharp corners, the pathway to the house should not lead directly from a corner but rather curve gently towards the house. A pa kua mirror over the front door will help deflect any negative influences.

Adding to sharp corners or blocking them off with vegetation or garden structures, such as a greenhouse or shed, lessens the knife-like effect and eases the flow of ch'i around the house.

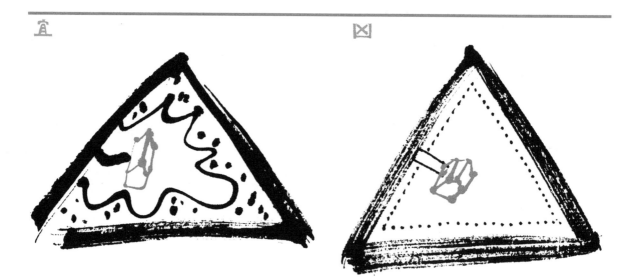

Soften the borders to create a curved effect, allowing ch'i to flow more smoothly. Trees or fencing can be used as shields, but be careful they are not so large that they overpower the house.

Avoid laying out gardens or paths with straight lines accentuating the angular shape, as these enable ch'i to move too quickly, and destructive energy will gather in the corners.

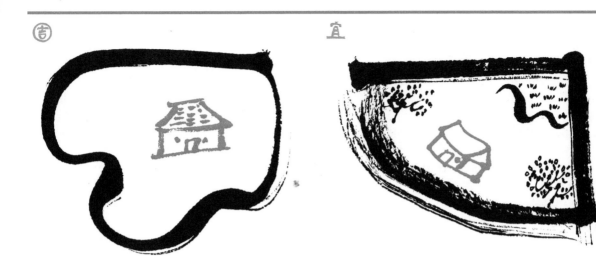

The curved borders enhance the flow of ch'i at the front. Although the shape is irregular, a balance is created, as the garden is in proportion to the size of the house.

The house faces a rounded edge, which is positive, and also has balanced space surrounding it, but it would help to strengthen the back corner with a border, shrubs or rounded gazebo.

Circular plots are good feng shui. There are no sharp corners to trap ch'i, and thus it is able to flow smoothly around the site, allowing it to be at its most beneficial.

If the house is located on a very small plot of land it can use the land and buildings on neighbouring plots to provide balance and support.

Assess the whole plot of a house or apartment block surrounded by buildings. Ideally the buildings should echo the animal spirit formation (see page 18).

Gardens

Vegetation provides life-giving ch'i and can enrich an area where ch'i may be slow-moving, dispersed or trapped. But vegetation can also dispel ch'i or limit its effects: for example, a high, dense collection of trees can create excess yin because of the dark, damp conditions around that site. Plants need to be used wisely to create balance and protection, to encourage ch'i and disperse sha.

When you are planning a garden, do not allow trees or shrubs to block out your light or disturb the foundations of your house. Shrubs and trees can, however, be extremely useful for providing protection in a weak area as well as for adding colour and shape to the design of your garden. Your garden plan may be relatively simple or it may be quite complex – for example, you might opt for a lawn surrounded on four sides by borders, or a garden that is broken into different sections to serve a variety of purposes. What is important is the cohesion and unity that it creates. Choose curved borders above straight or angular lines and use vegetation of different heights that blend well together, but always remember to clear away rotting vegetation or dead trees. If you are erecting a fence or a wall, grow plants up or close to it to gather further ch'i into the garden, and try to use garden furniture that is curved in shape or has rounded edges.

Round features or structures promote the smooth flow of ch'i. These include ponds, garden furniture, gazebos and rounded edging on lawns. Pools of water and fountains are ideally located at the front of the house to attract distant good fortune to the area. Gentle activity in the water, either caused by aquatic life or by the breeze, increases life-giving energy. Pools and ponds should be cleaned regularly to prevent water becoming stagnant and a source of destructive energy.

Do not allow structures or features in the garden to overwhelm the house or be out of proportion to the plot of land. If these features cannot be removed, use a mirror or a metal spring to deflect the pressure they place on the house. 'Greening' outbuildings with climbing plants or small shrubs softens sharp edges.

If you live in an L-shaped house, try to create a balance between the house and the open section by paving this area to create a patio or conservatory. Lamps, wall-lights or potted plants also help to activate ch'i in this area. The overall effect strengthens this open aspect and creates a symmetrical appearance.

Swimming pools have a strong yin nature that will overwhelm a house if too close to it; to avoid this, plant a screen of shrubs or build a low wall. The pool should be cleared of dead leaves or rotting vegetation to prevent sha settling over the pool and affecting the health of those using the pool or living in the house.

good feng shui   bad feng shui   improved feng shui

Higher trees and bushes should be positioned at the rear of the house to strengthen the Black Tortoise (although not planted too close to the house), with lower shrubs and flowerbeds to the front to support the Red Bird.

If you have a small courtyard or balcony, introduce greenery, flowers or climbing plants on the walls since healthy plants produce life-giving energy. Do not, however, allow trees to overshadow the building since they could exert pressure on the occupants.

The four guardian animals should be balanced in the garden just as they should be in the buildings around the house and the structure of the house itself. In the illustration (left), the density of trees on the White

Tiger side overpowers the flat, featureless lawn on the Green Dragon side. The height and size of the trees should be controlled and the Green Dragon should be strengthened with flowerbeds, shrubs and trees (right).

 good feng shui   bad feng shui   improved feng shui

If you have a small, enclosed, paved yard behind your house or apartment, do not allow garbage or other waste to be scattered across this space. Keep the garbage covered and away from the back door of the building. The surface of the paved area should be smooth, even if the pattern of the paving blocks is irregular, and flowers or low shrubs should be planted in the available border space. Climbing plants trained up the walls will also help to soften the effect of brick or wooden fences surrounding the yard. Plant pots are another means of introducing ch'i into this area — but keep the plants healthy, removing dead stems or flowers as necessary.

If you are creating a pathway through your garden, allow it to curve gently, and build up the vegetation gradually on either side. Put smaller, lower plants close to the path and the taller ones at the back of the border. Choose colours and textures that work in harmony with each other to create a balanced and relaxing impression.

The Shape of Your Home

Balance, proportion and protection are central factors when assessing the feng shui of your home. This section deals particularly with the shapes of buildings, whether they are detached houses, rows of terraced houses or apartment buildings. There is no absolute set of rules, since a building can accommodate a wide variety of shapes, textures and features and still maintain a sense of harmony.

Just as land is surrounded by four animal guardians, these guardians are also seen in the architecture of buildings. If several extra floors were built on the right-hand side of a building, the coordination between the White Tiger and the Green Dragon is disrupted since the White Tiger becomes too powerful and may devour the Green Dragon (*see illustration below*).

If one side of the house is taller or longer it should be on the side of the Green Dragon, since this is a productive spirit. Do not, however,

allow it to overwhelm the proportions of the building.

A building does not have to be perfectly symmetrical but it should be balanced – extra floors, extensions, porches, patios and unusual architectural features can all be incorporated into the design, but they should not overwhelm or weigh down one part of the building. Ideally, a house or apartment should have a greater depth than width to establish stability, although narrow buildings can gain support from the features surrounding the site.

Buildings should convey a sense of unity in their construction. If a building is disjointed, top-heavy or confusing to look at, then the occupants may also feel confused, tense or under pressure. In contrast, a well-proportioned house encourages life-giving ch'i thereby enhancing the well-being of the occupants as well as improving the feng shui of the immediate environment.

Green Dragon

White Tiger

To maintain the most positive balance the Green Dragon should be higher than the White Tiger, in order to control the Tiger's great energy.

Green Dragon

White Tiger

The White Tiger is a powerful and potentially destructive spirit if allowed to dominate a building. Springs and mirrors on the lower roof help disperse its power.

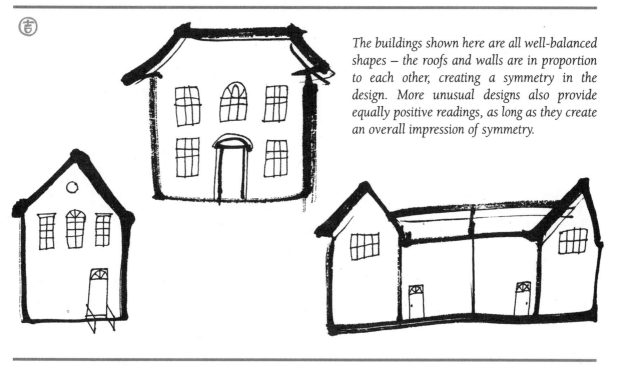

The buildings shown here are all well-balanced shapes – the roofs and walls are in proportion to each other, creating a symmetry in the design. More unusual designs also provide equally positive readings, as long as they create an overall impression of symmetry.

Extensions built in the roof should always be in proportion to the overall dimensions of the building.

An extension should not be allowed to overwhelm or overhang the house. A spring can be placed on the floor to bounce away the pressure created by the overhang.

Small terraces or balconies will not disturb the overall harmony. A small awning can serve as a useful gathering place for ch'i but it should not extend too far.

good feng shui   bad feng shui   improved feng shui

Extensions on the ground floor add support to the house as long as they are not too large in relation to the main structure, but extensions on the floors above could make the house top-heavy.

Extensions, conservatories or features of the house with domed roofs encourage the even flow of ch'i, since their round shape is complete and therefore a sign of fullness.

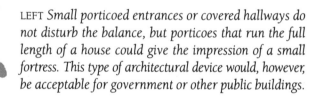

LEFT *Small porticoed entrances or covered hallways do not disturb the balance, but porticoes that run the full length of a house could give the impression of a small fortress. This type of architectural device would, however, be acceptable for government or other public buildings.*

BELOW *Small porches or extensions to single-storey buildings do not overwhelm the basic structure of the house. (If possible, try to incorporate rounded features in extensions.)*

good feng shui   bad feng shui   improved feng shui

Too many jagged features cut sharply through ch'i and can cause an unsettled atmosphere. Soften sharp angles with climbing plants or baskets; lights can also help to enliven ch'i.

A variety of sloping roofs and levels on a house could result in the occupants' profits rolling off. Rounded eaves or gutters will control this loss, and mirrors placed at the base of the slope will help to reflect it back.

If the size of the chimneys is out of proportion to the size of the house they dominate the building and pierce the space above, making them subject to destructive forces.

A large house or apartment block can accommodate a variety of unusual or different shapes if each of the design elements is well-proportioned, thereby creating an overall harmony. While this range of windows, bays and roof levels can sit easily on a larger house, do not cramp a small house with too great a variety of architectural detail.

The support on the left-hand side of this building is hollow and weak and makes it appear as though half the house is sitting on stilts. If possible, this weak section should be walled in, creating a porch or atrium. The room that lacks solid foundations should be used for storage rather than as a bedroom or study.

When the garage is an integral part of the house the car appears to be driving straight at the occupants. As the car moves into the house it cuts through the ch'i and disperses its beneficial effect. Avoid using the room directly behind or above the garage as a kitchen, living room or bedroom.

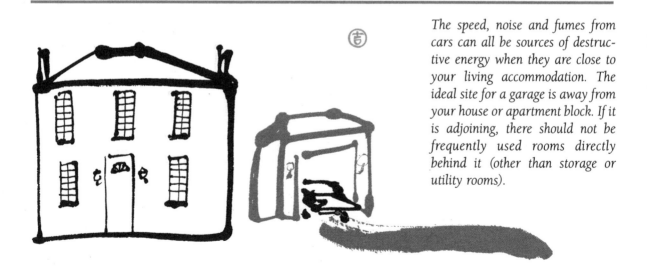

The speed, noise and fumes from cars can all be sources of destructive energy when they are close to your living accommodation. The ideal site for a garage is away from your house or apartment block. If it is adjoining, there should not be frequently used rooms directly behind it (other than storage or utility rooms).

good feng shui   bad feng shui   improved feng shui

The Front Door

The front door is the main access for ch'i into your home, so if ch'i is blocked or trapped at this point the occupants will not be able to benefit from its active and energizing qualities. Therefore, the main entrance to a building should not be enclosed on three sides or approached by narrow passageways. Similarly, the entrance to an apartment within an apartment block should not be in a cramped or badly-lit corridor.

If ch'i is funnelled towards the front door down arrow-like pathways, the impact on your home could be overwhelming. Paths that run steeply away from the front door result in good fortune rolling away from the house. It is important that ch'i is channelled evenly and freely towards the main entrance, while the door itself – the mouth of the house – should be well-maintained, upright and in proportion to the building.

A downward slope sends ch'i forcefully towards the front door – the low dip is also a place where negative energy can collect. Terracing this area can help to regulate the flow of ch'i.

The access to the front door is open and the gently sloping back garden offers protection, since it strengthens the guardian spirit of the Black Tortoise at the back of the house.

The access to the front door should be flat or sloping slightly upwards so that ch'i can flow smoothly towards the front door.

If the path leading to the front door slopes away from the house, a row of shrubs or small trees will help to slow ch'i running away from the site.

BELOW *A driveway that is wide in proportion to the size of the house funnels ch'i forcefully towards the front door. Dividing the drive into sections by placing shrubs or small trees at regular intervals will help to control ch'i's rapid approach.*

Lights on either side of the door will also help, as will an outdoor standing lamp, which will act as a guardian. Make sure that the lights are all working properly. Window blinds also help to shield the house from energy travelling down this wide path.

If the front door leads straight on to a busy main road, unpleasant traffic fumes and noise can adversely affect the health of the occupants. Shield the door or vulnerable windows with blinds or curtains, and activate ch'i with healthy plants, flowers or shrubs.

If the house is situated on a steep hill with the front door facing the road, erect a fence either side of the house to control the flow of chi. The fence on the right blocks the onrush of energy, the fence on the left contains some of the energy as it sweeps down the hill.

Ch'i can flow gently towards the house if the front path or driveway is evenly curved. Ideally, the driveway for a car should curve round towards the side of the house, and the footpath should lead from the driveway to the front door.

RIGHT *If the path leading to your house is long and straight, its arrow-like effect can be lessened with a gate, a screen of shrubs or a porch (particularly if the entrance is to the side). A pa kua mirror will also lessen the impact of negative energy.*

LEFT *If a road points straight at your house like a knife, control the onward rush of ch'i and sha from it by creating a curved pathway leading to your house. A mirror above the front door will help, since reflective objects are particularly effective against oncoming traffic.*

FAR LEFT *Y-shaped paths leading to the front door can cause confusion and indecision. Minimize the effect by blocking off one of the paths with shrubs; ch'i can then be channelled down one route.*

LEFT *A gap between two buildings directly facing a front door draws financial fortune away from the house – like a slice from a cake. Protect the front door with a barrier, but do not place trees or fencing too close to the house, or so high, that they oppress those living there.*

good feng shui   bad feng shui   improved feng shui

The front door should not be continually in the shadow of trees that obstruct the light and put pressure on those living inside. Cut any such trees back; however, there is no need to remove them completely unless the roots are undermining the foundations.

Avoid planting equally sized, large bushes or trees on either side of the front door, as they are said to resemble joss-sticks burning at either side of a grave. Make them different sizes or add more plants to one side to alter the effect.

Remove dead trees or decaying vegetation, and mend broken fences or sheds that are rotting. All of these items can be sources of destructive energy entering your home.

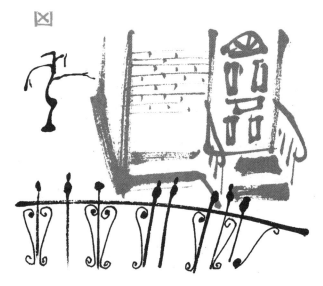

Do not place any rubbish bins or boxes of discarded waste around the front door, since sha accumulates here and will weaken the main access to the house or apartment.

LEFT *A corner of another building directly facing your front door is like a knife slicing into the house. Try to screen your front door and reflect or bounce back the cutting effect of this corner.*

RIGHT *A pool of water in the front garden attracts positive ch'i, but if too close to the front door it lets the strong yin nature of still water seep into the house. Water from a small stream or fountain should flow towards the house; if not, benevolent energy will be carried away.*

The front door, or porch around it, should not be out of proportion to the rest of the house. If the door is too large the onrush of ch'i is too strong, making the house vulnerable to negative energy. In contrast, if the front door is too small in proportion to the size of the house, the access for enriching ch'i is limited.

A house with two main entrances is like a face with two mouths – the flow of ch'i is divided and the occupants cannot receive the full benefit, as they would from a single flow of energy. Do not use one of the entrances, and design the other door so that it is obvious which is the main access.

Make sure the front door is hung straight and that it is free of rot or damp. If the hinges and locks creak or squeal, oil them so the noise does not disturb the equilibrium of the home.

good feng shui   bad feng shui   improved feng shui

Inside the Home

Your health, relationships and work can all be affected by the flow of ch'i through your home or by the build-up of negative forces in certain areas. The living room, dining room and bedroom are traditionally regarded as the three most important rooms in the house since you relax, eat and sleep in these rooms. Nothing should be taken in isolation, however, and if the feng shui in these three rooms is ideal but the remaining rooms are overcrowded, dark, cramped or badly maintained, this will reverberate in other parts of your home.

When assessing your home it is helpful to start by analysing an overall floor plan using your Pa Tzu compass. You can then work your way through the rooms to check whether any improvements are necessary. For example, are there corners or angles where negative energy could accumulate? Do any minor adjustments need to be made to the furniture or fabrics? Using your Pa Tzu compass within individual rooms enables you to discover where the elements are unbalanced and lack harmony. And handy checklists for each room remind you of what to look for when you make your assessment. (Please note: for guidelines for a study, refer to the section on workplace layout on page 122.)

You may find that there is already a feeling of equilibrium and peace in your home, or that you sense a beneficial flow of energy and therefore nothing needs to be corrected or altered. Feng shui principles and suggestions for improvement are given, but these are not absolute rules and you should follow your judgement.

How to Analyse Your Apartment Floor Plan

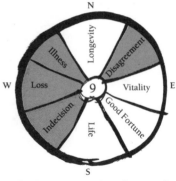

Before you can carry out your reading you need to know which of the eight Pa Tzu compasses belongs to your year of birth. You can discover the number of your compass, your lucky and unlucky directions and your personal element by referring to pages 24–6.

We have used Pa Tzu compass number 9 (*see right*) in the reading given below. The element for this compass is fire. Work through the example and apply the same technique to your own floor plan with your personal Pa Tzu compass.

Pa Tzu compass 9 • Element: fire

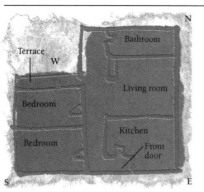

ABOVE *Scale drawing of apartment floor plan.*

BELOW *Overlaying your Pa Tzu compass on your floor plan.*

1 OVERLAYING YOUR COMPASS Draw a floor plan of your apartment (or each floor of your home) to scale and overlay your Pa Tzu compass, as explained on pages 26–7 (*see left and below left*). Remember to align north on the compass with the northern direction of your apartment. Alternatively, use the compass printed in this book and stand in the centre of your home, pointing north on your compass towards north in your apartment.

Your Pa Tzu compass only has one element associated with it, but the eight directions of your apartment each have their own element. Whether you are doing a reading of the floor plan of a room or a house, these directions and their associated elements do not change.

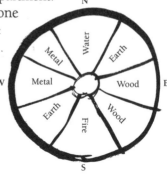

Directions and associated elements.

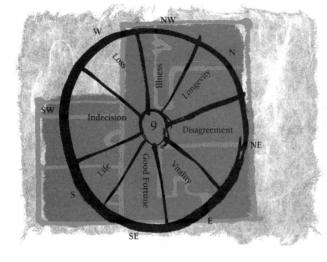

2 ASSESSING THE ELEMENTS You can see from our floor plan (*left*) that the four unlucky directions are in the north-west, west, south-west and north-east, and these are the areas that need attention. Since the element that belongs to Pa Tzu compass number 9 is fire, you need to find out fire's relationship with metal and earth – the elements associated with the four unlucky directions in this example (*see floor plan on next page*). Look at the productive and destructive cycles of the elements shown opposite.

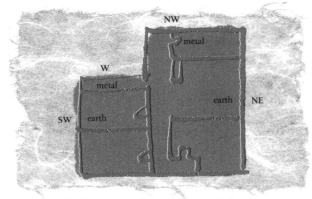

The unlucky directions and their associated elements.

3 WORKING THROUGH UNLUCKY DIRECTIONS Work through each of your unlucky directions and its relationship with your personal element – in this case, fire – one step at a time.

❌ *The north-west and west fall into the categories of Illness and Loss. The element associated with both these directions is metal. The table below shows that fire destroys metal.*

This is a positive reading, since the powerful action of fire overcomes metal and improves the negative readings of these directions. Since fire is a very powerful element you do not need to strengthen it further.

❌ *The south-west and north-east fall into the categories of Indecision and Disagreement. The element associated with both these directions is earth. The table below shows that fire produces earth in productive cycle.*

This is an effective combination, since fire is in harmony with earth. If you want to strengthen the creative action of fire in the bedroom or living-room area you can introduce various shades of red or orange into your colour scheme, as well as installing additional lighting or hanging paintings that depict fire. Do not, however, allow the fire element to become overwhelming. *(See also pages 22–3.)*

4 APARTMENT LAYOUT The main entrance and the kitchen are both in favourable positions: the main route of ch'i into the home is through the front door, which falls into the Good Fortune section, and the kitchen – which produces the family's nourishment – is located in the Vitality section.

To ensure that ch'i can enter smoothly through the front door, check that the door is well-maintained and in proportion to the front aspect of the apartment. You should also remember to take into account the position of the front door in relation to outside features such as sharp corners, gaps, or dark or overcrowded areas. Once ch'i has entered the home it needs space to establish its flow in order to ensure adequate circulation to other rooms. In our apartment it is allowed sufficient space, but it would be funnelled into the house through a cramped, narrow corridor or if the doors to the bedroom and living room were very close to the front door.

In this example the bathroom is at the back of the apartment, away from the kitchen and with its doorway leading into the hall rather than directly into another room. It is in a strong position, since it is separate from the source of food and away from the living area. If there is only one door leading in and out of the apartment, however, there is a danger that germs could get trapped at the end of the hallway, making the ch'i sluggish and thereby encouraging sha. Try to create an even circulation of air and keep this area free of clutter or waste; introducing adequate lighting will also help to keep ch'i active.

Productive cycle	Destructive cycle
wood produces fire	wood destroys earth
fire produces earth	earth destroys water
earth produces metal	water destroys fire
metal produces water	fire destroys metal
water produces wood	metal destroys wood

The Hall and Stairs

Once ch'i has entered your home it needs sufficient space to circulate freely so it can be evenly distributed throughout the rooms. If ch'i is blocked at this initial stage its flow is disrupted and its beneficial effect weakened. Cramped or dark halls and stairways also encourage the accumulation of negative energy, which becomes trapped. Do not overcrowd halls or stairs with unnecessary furniture or objects, and if natural light cannot enter make sure the area is well-lit and brightly decorated.

The front door should not open directly on to to the stairs, since the rush of ch'i entering will be directed away from the ground floor; this design could also provide a route for ch'i to roll out of the building. Ch'i needs space and light to adjust and circulate on first entering the house or apartment; beneficial conditions here also diminish the effect of negative forces that may be channelled or reflected towards your home.

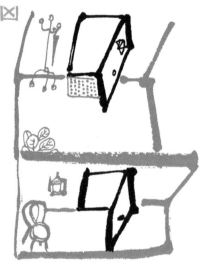

If the front door opens on to a dark, confined area, the circulation of ch'i into the main body of the house or apartment is cramped. Enliven the ch'i in this space with a healthy green-leafed plant, bright wall colours and a mirror (but do not place the mirror directly opposite the front door). In very dark hallways, a light should be kept on at all times.

The hallway or lobby is the main access for ch'i into the house or apartment, so the area should be kept clear of waste, crowded furniture and sharp, angular objects. Create light, spacious conditions to encourage the efficient circulation of energy in the rest of the home. The activity of wind chimes above the door also enlivens ch'i in this space.

If the front door opens directly on to a door leading into another room, do not open both doors at once, to prevent an overwhelming rush of ch'i into the house or apartment. A small entrance space, such as the one shown above, should also be kept clean, clear of clutter and well-lit.

 good feng shui   bad feng shui   improved feng shui

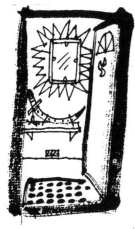

LEFT *Avoid placing mirrors or knife-like ornaments directly opposite the front door, since they will reflect or cut through the incoming ch'i. (If you need to counteract negative forces here, use a small ornamental mirror.)*

ABOVE *If the front door opens directly on to a staircase there is nothing to block or disperse negative energy entering the upper floors of the building. This design also enables ch'i to rush in, or down the stairs and travel straight out of the door. Do not leave the front door open, and create a screen with a large green-leafed plant or a piece of furniture. If, however, the house is very small and the stairs are part of the living room, ch'i will be able to reach the ground floor.*

Stairs should be gently rising and evenly spaced with sufficient room at the foot of the stairs and on the landing for ch'i to become established and then circulate to other rooms and apartments. If the door of your room or apartment is very close to a flight of stairs, place a mirror over the door to deflect any negative forces.

Checklist

• Does the front door open into a bright, uncluttered space?
• Does the front door open directly in line with an inner door?
• Is there enough room in the hall or lobby for the smooth circulation of ch'i into the rest of the building?
• Is there adequate lighting in the hall or lobby?
• Is there a stairway close to the front door?
• Is the staircase cramped, narrow or poorly lit?
• Is there a landing at the top of the staircase?

Ch'i can be channelled too forcefully up narrow, straight stairs or unevenly dispersed on winding, irregular stairs. If you cannot alter the layout of the stairs, make sure that the area is clean, brightly lit and well decorated. Although mirrors can be used to deflect the flow of negative forces, do not hang one so that your head is cut off in the reflection. Greenery, lamps, flowers or pictures of landscapes can also be used to encourage beneficial energy.

The Living Room

The living room or sitting room is usually the place where family and friends gather, so you need to create an environment that is conducive to relaxation and conversation. If the living room leads directly on to the street or if several doors lead into the room, it can leave you feeling vulnerable. In contrast, a dark, confined living area creates oppressive conditions.

Arrange your furniture to provide protection from the rush of energy that can enter through a doorway or large window, and do not face sharp corners or angular objects – they cut through beneficial energy. The sofa is usually the item of furniture used most frequently; therefore it needs particular support from a wall or from another piece of furniture (the same principle applies for armchairs). As well as the seating arrangements remember to take into account the height of the room – if the ceiling is too high in proportion to the size of the room, ch'i rises and disperses, but if the ceiling is too low, ch'i is condensed and cramped. Do not put chairs under a beam: this could cause financial ruin or ill health. If the room if full of alcoves and corners energy, may be caught and trapped, so do not clutter these areas. In most cases, you can take appropriate measures to encourage a more efficient flow of ch'i through the use of colour, lights, plants, reflective objects, blinds, screens and furniture arrangement (*see also pages 28–33*).

Ideally the front door should not lead straight into the living room. This is acceptable if the house or apartment is small, but if the living room is large, block the force of the incoming ch'i with a screen, bookcase or partition.

If the kitchen and living room are open-plan, try to screen off the kitchen area to prevent smells and steam filling the area where you sit and relax. Clear away left-over food and empty the kitchen waste bins regularly.

 good feng shui   bad feng shui   improved feng shui

The design of the living room should create an easy, relaxing atmosphere. Try to organize lights so they enhance this; do not use bright fluorescent tubes or bulbs directly above your head, since they may cause headaches and nausea. Avoid crowding the room with ornaments, sharp objects and angular furniture — ch'i moves more freely around curved edges and symmetrical arrangements.

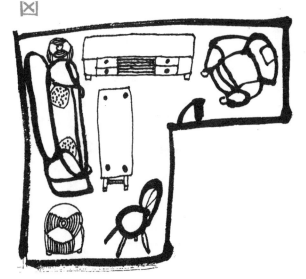

Do not create cramped passageways between furniture, since it funnels negative forces and limits the circulation of ch'i. If your living room is L-shaped, do not crowd the narrower part of the room with furniture or ornaments, and place lamps in dark corners.

Too much ch'i can escape through large windows or patio doors, particularly if they are opposite each other. Make use of blinds or curtains to control the loss of energy. The reading is, however, improved if the windows are divided into smaller panes of glass.

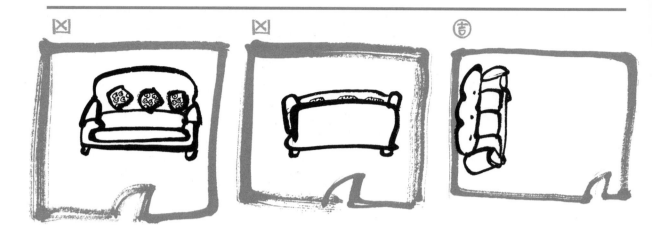

Avoid placing the sofa directly opposite the door since it receives a rush of ch'i as the door opens and is directly in the line of negative forces entering the room. The impact of ch'i can leave you feeling drained and vulnerable.

Do not leave yourself unprotected by placing the back of the sofa directly in line with the door. If this arrangement is unavoidable, wind chimes over the door would alert you to someone entering the room.

Ideally the sofa should have the support of a wall behind it. This position allows you to feel secure and in control, since you are able to see who is entering or leaving the room.

If the sofa is in the middle of the room, try to create some support behind you with a low bookcase, shelving unit or screen.

A place where you pray or meditate should be distanced from noisy areas, open doors or overhead beams. If space is limited, find a clean, peaceful corner in your living room where you are unlikely to be disturbed.

 good feng shui   ⊠ bad feng shui   ⛩ improved feng shui

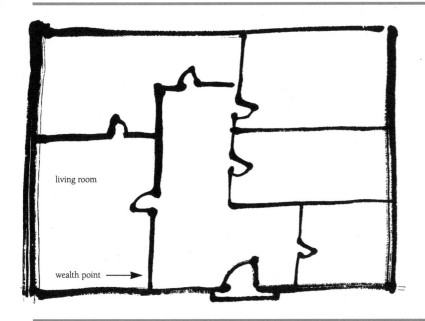

living room

wealth point →

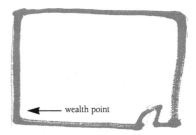

← wealth point

There is a part of the living room popularly known as the 'wealth point'. It is said to be in the top left-hand corner, directly to your left rather than opposite, as you enter the room. If there are two doors into the room, the wealth point relates to the door leading from the front of your home.

A doorway or arch in the wealth point creates a passageway for good financial fortune to slip through. Steam from a kettle or coffee-maker at this point will also draw money away.

Any doors at the wealth point should be kept closed. An archway should be covered by a screen or sliding doors. A plant with large, rounded, green leaves can enliven ch'i in this area. (Remember to remove any dead leaves or shoots.)

Checklist

• Is the sofa (and/or armchairs) supported and protected?
• Are there doors opening in line with one another?
• Is there too little light in the room?
• Are there very bright overhead lights?
• Is the flow of ch'i limited by cluttered furniture or ornaments?
• Are there many sharp corners or angular features?
• Do the windows need blinds for protection?
• Is there a lavatory door opening directly into the room?
• Is the sofa positioned under a beam?
• Is there an eating area close to the area where you relax?

How to Analyse Your Living-room Floor Plan

Before you can carry out your reading you need to know which of the eight Pa Tzu compasses belongs to your year of birth. You can discover the number of your compass, your lucky and unlucky directions and your personal element by referring to pages 24–6.

We have used Pa Tzu compass number 2 (*see right*) in the example given below. The element for this compass is earth. Work through the example and then apply the same technique to your own living-room floor plan, using your personal Pa Tzu compass.

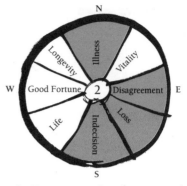

Pa Tzu compass 2 • Element: earth

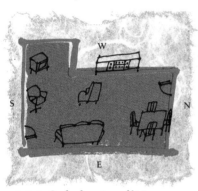

ABOVE *Scale drawing of living-room floor plan.*

BELOW *Overlaying your Pa Tzu compass on your floor plan.*

1 OVERLAYING YOUR COMPASS Draw a floor plan of your living room to scale and overlay your Pa Tzu compass, as explained on pages 26–7 (*see left and below left*). Remember to align north on your compass with the northern direction of your living room. If you prefer, you can simply use the compass printed in this book and stand in the centre of your living room, pointing north on your compass towards north in your living room.

Your Pa Tzu compass only has one element associated with it, but the eight directions of your living room each have their own element. Whether you are doing a reading of the floor plan of a room or of a house, these directions and their associated elements do not change.

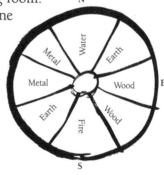

Directions and associated elements.

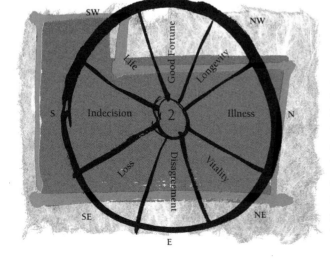

2 ASSESSING THE ELEMENTS You can see from our floor plan (*left*) that the four unlucky directions are in the south, south-east, east and north, and these are the areas that need attention. Since the element that belongs to Pa Tzu compass 2 is earth, you need to find earth's relationship with fire, wood and water – the elements associated with the four unlucky directions in this example (*see floor plan on next page*). Look at the productive and destructive cycles of the elements shown opposite.

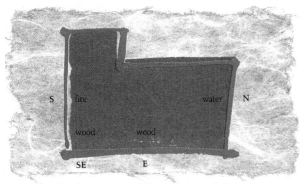

The unlucky directions and their associated elements.

3 WORKING THROUGH UNLUCKY DIRECTIONS Work through each of your unlucky directions and its relationship with your personal element – in this case, earth – one step at a time.

☒ *South falls into the category of Indecision. The element associated with south is fire. The table below shows that fire produces earth.*

This is a good reading, since your element works in harmony with fire. The energy of fire is used to form earth, and in the process fire is drained as it nourishes and strengthens earth.

☒ *South-east and east fall into the categories of Loss and Disagreement. The element associated with both these directions is wood. From the table we can see that wood destroys earth.*

Since your element is overpowered by wood you have to find out which element weakens or drains wood. Wood produces fire, so the energy of wood is drained as it works to nourish and create fire. If you introduce the fire element through colours, textures or fabrics, the power of wood is channelled and will be weakened. You can use sources of heat such as real or gas fires, objects or paintings that depict fire, or warm colours with red or orange hues (*see also pages 22–3*).

The cycles of elements also show that wood is overcome by metal. When you use the destructive cycle, do not let one element attack another too forcefully. You could introduce metal ornaments, picture frames or incorporate metal into furniture. Shades of white or cream can also be put to good effect in fabrics, paintings or colour schemes. But do not overwhelm the room with one element, as this disturbs the overall balance.

☒ *North falls into the category of Illness. The element associated with north is water. From the table we can see that earth destroys water.*

In this combination earth controls water and thereby strengthens the reading for this direction. You do not need to increase earth as it is already strong. If you want to weaken the water element, channel it towards fire, since water is depleted as it destroys fire, and fire, in turn, strengthens earth. Do not overwhelm the area with fire, however, as you are working with the elements that overpower each other in the destructive cycle.

4 ROOM LAYOUT Examine the position of furniture and doors in your unlucky areas. In our example the sofa is in the Loss and Disagreement areas, but the back of the sofa offers protection; when you sit here you face Life, Good Fortune and Longevity. The position of the sofa is particularly important, as this is the place where household members talk and relax. Similarly, armchairs can be used to add support if their backs are to a wall in a weak area. The left and right doors open into Loss and Illness, but these areas can be strengthened using the elemental combinations described above. The table and chairs are in the Vitality area, so this is a positive place for eating, conversation or study (keep the door closed to avoid being in the path of ch'i entering or leaving the room).

Productive cycle	Destructive cycle
wood produces fire	wood destroys earth
fire produces earth	earth destroys water
earth produces metal	water destroys fire
metal produces water	fire destroys metal
water produces wood	metal destroys wood

The Kitchen

For many people the kitchen is more than a room to store and prepare food – it is also the place to meet, eat, play, discuss ideas or difficulties. This is why the kitchen is regarded as a 'treasure', since it is the place that nourishes the family. It also traditionally reflects the fortunes of the family, since the quality of the food indicates the family's prosperity.

If the house is compared to the human body, the kitchen is associated with the stomach – if the positioning and layout of the kitchen is harmonious, then the health and well-being of the family will also be balanced.

In ancient China, the most auspicious site for a kitchen was the east, away from the south-facing front door and in line with the south-easterly winds that were useful for igniting fuel.

In time, the south and the east became the traditional directions for a kitchen, since they also link in with the creative cycle of the five elements. Fire is the element associated with the south, and wood with the east; fire was need to cook food and wood was the element needed to produce fire.

Today, kitchens are not orientated to any particular direction. However, it is important that the beneficial ch'i that may be present in this area does not quickly escape through doors that open in line with one another, or decay because of dark or unhygienic conditions. Since food is usually prepared using the cooker, particular attention is paid to its position, so that support and protection is provided for both the cooker and the cook.

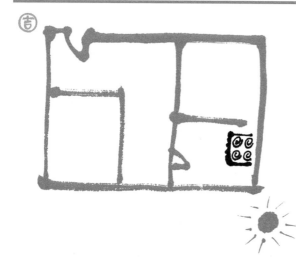

The south and south-eastern sides of the house are traditionally the most favourable directions for a kitchen. Of more importance in modern kitchens are the circulation of ch'i, the arrangement of units and furniture, an adequate amount of light and ventilation, and a good level of hygiene.

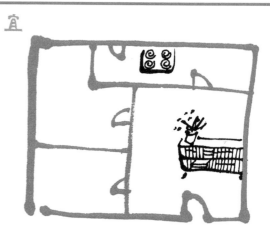

The kitchen should not be directly in line with the front door. In addition to beneficial ch'i escaping, negative energy can travel directly to this important family room. You can form a barrier with a bookcase or unit of furniture, but if this is impossible do not leave the front and kitchen doors open at the same time.

 good feng shui   ⊠ bad feng shui   improved feng shui

When ch'i is circulating through the house or apartment, it should be able to flow smoothly towards the kitchen (far left). If energy is hindered by twisting passageways and steps or long dark corridors, its flow is disrupted and its beneficial effect weakened (left). Keep these areas well-lit, and use a mirror to counteract the effect of sharp corners.

BELOW *Since the kitchen is central to the health and prosperity of those who live in the building, it needs support and protection. If the kitchen is in a room that juts out to form an extension from the main body of the house, it is like a limb attached a body when it should be part of the trunk. If the kitchen is unprotected on three sides, the support will have to be provided from features outside, such as neighbouring walls, fences, bushes and trees.*

ABOVE *Ideally the kitchen should have more than one door, to prevent ch'i becoming trapped and drained as it circles around the enclosed space. Natural light, clear glass windows, ventilation fans and other moving objects all help to encourage a more efficient and smooth flow of ch'i in, around and out of the room. If your kitchen has no external window, effective ventilation and lighting become even more important.*

The entrance to the kitchen should not be directly in line with the back door of the house or apartment, since ch'i entering the kitchen could pass rapidly through. Try to divert its flow by placing furniture or kitchen units in this space. To prevent a forceful rush of energy, avoid leaving both doors open.

The kitchen should not be opposite or next to the lavatory, since germs and odours may spread into the area where food is prepared. If this arrangement is unavoidable, and the two rooms are close to each other, keep lavatory door closed and keep the lavatory itself well-ventilated.

Do not block access to the kitchen with piles of papers, bags or other household objects, which break the flow of ch'i. If the corridor leading to the kitchen is long and dark, decorate it with bright colours and use lights, greenery, landscape images or pictures depicting peaceful activity to enliven ch'i.

Do not obstruct movement in the kitchen with too much furniture or with cluttered objects. The path of ch'i can be disrupted or trapped in crowded and untidy places. The kitchen should be a bright and healthy place, so avoid the build-up of garbage, piles of newspaper, unwashed laundry or dishes and other obstacles that might inhibit the flow of ch'i. If the kitchen waste is not disposed of on a regular basis, sha enters and drains the life-giving energy that should be present in this room.

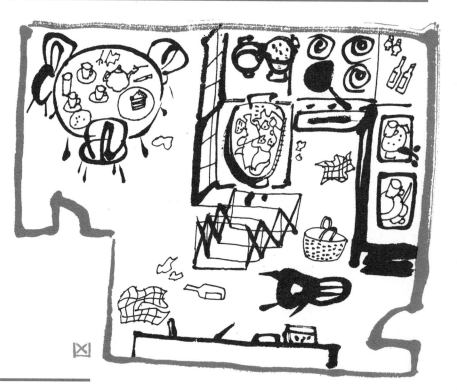

Position the cooker so it is away from the direct line of the door. If you are standing at the cooker with your back to the door, not only do you lack support but are unable to see who is entering or leaving. You can improve your sense of security by adding chimes above the door so you are aware of any movement there.

The cooker should not be positioned under a window, since the food may deteriorate if exposed to sunlight. In addition, the cooker itself lacks support in front. If you cannot move the cooker, keep the blinds down or curtains partially drawn when you are cooking.

Do not leave knives or other sharp objects hanging from the units. In addition to being a potential health hazard they also cut through the ch'i of the kitchen. When they are not in use, keep them in drawers or place them in a knife rack.

Avoid placing the cooker next to the sink or the fridge, since the fire element of the cooker is overpowered by the water element present in these cold, wet areas. Place a panel, table or saucepan storage unit between the two to create a barrier.

Checklist

• Is the kitchen directly in line with the front door of the house?
• Is the flow of ch'i to the kitchen hindered by dark or twisting corridors?
• Are knives or other sharp objects hanging from the kitchen units?
• Is the kitchen well-lit and well-ventilated?
• Is movement in the kitchen limited by furniture or clutter?
• Is the kitchen opposite or adjoining the lavatory?
• Is the cooker positioned under a window?
• Can you see who is entering or leaving the room when you are using the cooker?

good feng shui   bad feng shui   improved feng shui

How to Analyse Your Kitchen Floor Plan

Before you can carry out your reading you need to know which of the eight Pa Tzu compasses belongs to your year of birth. You can discover the number of your compass, your lucky and unlucky directions and your personal element by referring to pages 24–6.

We have used Pa Tzu compass number 4 (*see right*) in the reading given below. The element for this compass is wood. Work through the example and then apply the same technique to your own kitchen floor plan, using your personal Pa Tzu compass.

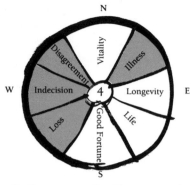

Pa Tzu compass 4 • Element: wood

ABOVE *Scale drawing of kitchen floor plan.*

BELOW *Overlaying your Pa Tzu compass on your floor plan.*

1 OVERLAYING YOUR COMPASS Draw a floor plan of your kitchen to scale and overlay your Pa Tzu compass, as explained on pages 26–7 (*see left and below left*). Remember to align north on your compass with the northern direction of your kitchen. Alternatively, simply use the compass printed in this book and stand in the centre of your kitchen, pointing north on the compass towards north in your kitchen.

Your Pa Tzu compass only has one element associated with it, but the eight directions of your kitchen each have their own element. Whether you are doing a reading of the floor plan of a room or a house, these directions and their associated elements do not change.

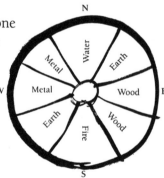

Directions and associated elements.

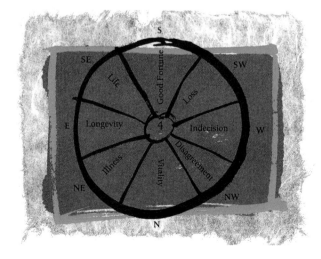

2 ASSESSING THE ELEMENTS You can see from our floor plan (*left*) that the four unlucky directions are in the west, north-west, south-west and north-east, and these are the areas that need attention. Since the element that belongs to Pa Tzu compass number 4 is wood, you need to find wood's relationship with earth and metal – the elements associated with the four unlucky directions in this example (*see floor plan on next page*). Look at the productive and destructive cycles of the elements shown opposite.

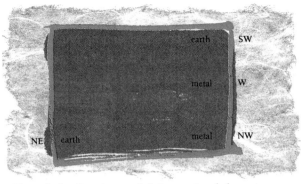

The unlucky directions and their associated elements.

3 WORKING THROUGH UNLUCKY DIRECTIONS Work through each of your unlucky directions and its relationship with your personal element – in this case, wood – one step at a time.

☒ *West and north-west fall into the categories of Indecision and Disagreement. The element associated with these two directions is metal. From the table you can see that metal destroys wood.*

Your element is overpowered by metal, so you need to find out which element weakens or drains metal. Metal produces water, and as it works to nourish water its power is dissipated. As water gains strength it then works to produce wood, which is your personal element. In order to strengthen water, introduce water colours or textures or water itself. Although black is the colour linked to water, do not overpower the kitchen with black but incorporate it through black cooking pots or pans, cooking utensils or tones in curtains, blinds or flooring; these will all help to channel metal towards the water element. Water itself is usually already strong in kitchens because of sinks, washing machines and fridges, so you may simply need to add a glass vase of flowers.

Metal is also dissolved when it has to work to destroy wood; therefore an increase in wood textures or colours will make metal work harder and in this destructive process its power is weakened.

If you look at the destructive cycle of elements you will also see that metal is destroyed by fire. Fire is a powerful element by nature and you should use it carefully. Since this reading is for a kitchen, the fire element is present in a gas or electric cooker, so it is unlikely that you will need to strengthen it further.

☒ *South-west and north-east fall into the categories of Loss and Illness. The element associated with both these directions is earth. From the table below you can see that wood destroys earth.*

Your personal element is already powerful and overwhelms earth, so you do not need to increase wood colours or textures in these areas.

4 ROOM LAYOUT The eating area in the east of this kitchen has a strong reading, since it falls into the categories of Life and Longevity. Anyone sitting at the table is also able to see who is entering through the back door, which provides a sense of security. One of the chairs, however, has its back to the inside door, so if you are sitting here keep this door closed for protection. If you are eating or working alone at this kitchen table, the chairs with the strongest support are those with their backs to the wall.

The west side of the kitchen has the weakest readings, but these can be strengthened through the elemental combinations above. The reading is helped by the fact that the cooker has the support of a wall in front and is not positioned next to the sink and fridge. Although you are working to improve the water element in this reading, the powerful water element present in the sink and fridge should not overwhelm the fire of the cooker.

Productive cycle	Destructive cycle
wood produces fire	wood destroys earth
fire produces earth	earth destroys water
earth produces metal	water destroys fire
metal produces water	fire destroys metal
water produces wood	metal destroys wood

The Bedroom

Rest and relaxation are vital for your general health, and the quality of sleep you attain affects the harmony of the house and relationships between the occupants. This is why the feng shui of bedrooms is important. The main bedroom has particular significance, since the occupants who usually sleep here are the main source of the household income.

Although the design of the room and the features within it all need consideration, the position of the bed is most important. You are at your most vulnerable when you are asleep, which is why the bed should be protected. If the bed is positioned behind the door you have no control over who is leaving or entering; if you sleep under a large window the ch'i entering or leaving the room may be too powerful; if you sleep under beams or at a place where the roof rises to a point, you could be subject to headaches, nervous disorders or general lack of energy. If the bed is in an alcove or there are shelves directly above the head of the bed, you may feel under pressure or claustrophobic.

Ideally the head of the bed needs support from a wall and should be away from the direct line of the door. Avoid creating cramped or oppressive conditions by cluttering the room with furniture, ornaments, books, papers or full waste-baskets. The use of light, textures and colours in this room should also contribute to creating a tranquil environment, so you gain maximum benefit from the circulation of ch'i.

RIGHT *If the bedroom is opposite or connected to the kitchen or bathroom, keep the doors closed to avoid steam, smells or germs spreading into the bedroom.*

BELOW *If the door opens on to your bed your energy could be drained; a set of drawers can act as a barrier.*

96

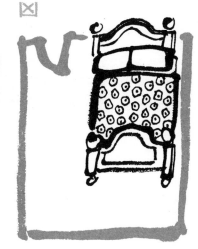

Do not hang or place a mirror directly opposite the foot of the bed, since you may be shocked if you wake up unexpectedly in the night and see your reflection.

For comfortable and secure sleep the bed head needs support and protection. If the bed is in an open space, support the head with a small screen or item of furniture, but do not put heavy objects on it or allow it to jut out over the bed.

If the head of the bed is behind the door, you have no control over who is entering the room. This leaves you in a vulnerable position. Placing wind chimes above the door will help to increase your sense of security.

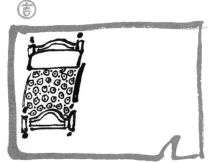

LEFT AND ABOVE *When the bed is in either of these positions, you can see who is entering the room and still be out of the direct line of the open door. This position offers a level of protection, since you are removed from an onrush of energy.*

Do not place very bright lights over the head of the bed since they disturb the equilibrium of the room and are said to cause eyesight or liver problems. Use soft colours and gentle lighting to create a feeling of tranquillity.

good feng shui   bad feng shui   improved feng shui

Exposed beams and rafters carry the weight of the house and put pressure on anyone sleeping directly underneath them. A beam that runs the length of the bed may cause headaches or nervous disorders. The beam could be covered by a false ceiling or you could hang a small reflective object from the beam to help disperse this pressure.

An exposed beam running across the middle of the bed is said to cause stomach disorders, while a beam crossing the foot of the bed could result in swelling of the feet. Reflective objects will help to disperse this pressure or small springs under the beam will help to bounce it back.

Do not obstruct the flow of ch'i under the bed by over-crowding this space with shoes, bags or other belong-ings. When the area under the bed is blocked, it could create dampness or cause backache.

Do not place the bed directly under a ceiling fan or large light fitting, since it creates the feeling that the large objects are about to fall on the person sleeping below, resulting in disturbed sleep.

good feng shui   bad feng shui   improved feng shui

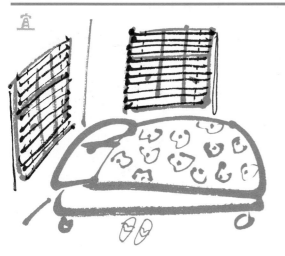

Avoid placing the bed directly under or beside a large window – not only is there a lack of protection but the amount of ch'i coming through the windows may disturb your sleep. If the bed cannot be moved, keep the blinds or curtains closed while you are resting.

Do not place a mirror directly opposite the bedroom window. The beneficial effects of ch'i are maximized when it circulates freely and smoothly, but a large mirror opposite the window will reflect back forcefully the incoming ch'i.

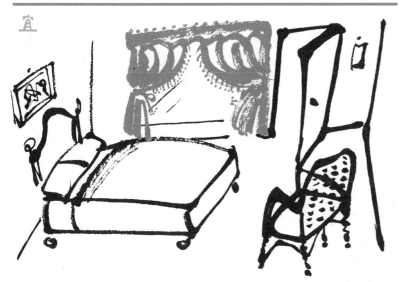

Windows with one pane of glass should not be larger than the door. When the powerful ch'i coming from the window is combined with the ch'i coming from the door, the total effect can be overwhelming. Window blinds or half-closed curtains help to reduce this impact. (If windows are divided into smaller panes of glass, the flow of ch'i is diffused.)

Checklist

• Is there direct access to the bathroom or kitchen from the bedroom?
• Is the entrance to the bedroom clear of clutter and furniture?
• Is the bed positioned out of the direct line of the door?
• Is there support behind the head of the bed?
• Is the bed positioned under a window?
• Is there a beam running across the foot of the bed or over the top of the bed?
• Is there a bright light or bookcase over the head of the bed?
• Is there a mirror opposite the foot of the bed?

How to Analyse Your Bedroom Floor Plan

Before you can carry out your reading you need to know which of the eight Pa Tzu compasses belongs to your year of birth. You can discover the number of your compass, your lucky and unlucky directions and your personal element by referring to pages 24–6.

We have used Pa Tzu compass number 7 *(see right)* in the reading given below. The element for this compass is metal. Work through the example and then apply the same technique to your own bedroom floor plan, using your personal Pa Tzu compass.

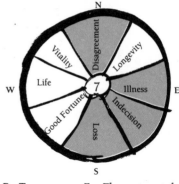

Pa Tzu compass 7 • Element: metal

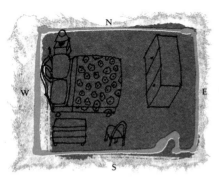

ABOVE *Scale drawing of bedroom floor plan.*

BELOW *Overlaying your Pa Tzu compass on your floor plan.*

I OVERLAYING YOUR COMPASS Draw a floor plan of your bedroom to scale and overlay your Pa Tzu compass, as explained on pages 26–7 *(see left and below left)*. Remember to align north on your compass with the northern direction of your bedroom. Or you can simply use the compass printed in this book and stand in the centre of your bedroom, pointing north on the compass towards north in your bedroom.

Your Pa Tzu compass only has one element associated with it, but the eight directions of your bedroom each have their own element. Whether you are doing a reading of the floor plan of a room or a house, these directions and their associated elements do not change.

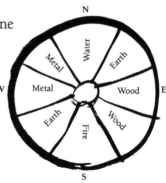

Directions and associated elements.

2 ASSESSING THE ELEMENTS You can see from our floor plan *(left)* that the four unlucky directions are in the east, south-east, south and north, and these are the areas that need attention. Since the element that belongs to Pa Tzu compass number 7 is metal, you need to find metal's relationship with wood, fire and water – the elements associated with the four unlucky directions in this example *(see floor plan on next page)*. Look at the productive and destructive cycles of the elements shown opposite.

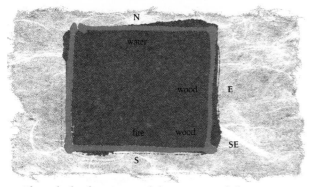

The unlucky directions and their associated elements.

3 WORKING THROUGH UNLUCKY DIRECTIONS Work through each of your unlucky directions and its relationship with your personal element – in this case, metal – one step at a time.

⊠ *East and south-east fall into the categories of Indecision and Illness. The element associated with both of these directions is wood. The table below shows that metal destroys wood.*

In this reading your personal element controls the power of wood and you do not need to strengthen it further.

⊠ *South falls into the category of Loss. The element associated with south is fire. The table below shows that fire destroys metal.*

Fire is strong in this combination and therefore needs to be controlled or dissolved to weaken its destructive qualities. By introducing more of your personal element, metal, through metal ornaments and frames, or tones of white, you can make fire work harder and thereby weaken itself (do not make the room completely white, as this resembles a hospital, representing ill health). Fire can be dissipated by making it produce earth, so if you introduce yellow hues or flowers into the room, fire's energy can be focused towards earth. Alternatively, since water destroys fire, tones of black could be used in fabrics, picture frames or ornaments, or scenes of gently flowing water could be depicted in drawings or photographs. *(See also pages 22–3.)*

⊠ *North falls into the category of Disagreement. The element associated with north is water. The table below shows that metal produces water.*

Your personal element works creatively with water, and though you can increase metal's effectiveness through metal ornaments, clocks or tones of white you do not need to make it too powerful.

4 ROOM LAYOUT The position of the bed is the most important aspect of any bedroom, since sleep and relaxation are vital to physical and emotional health. In this example the bed has a positive reading since it falls into the categories of Good Fortune, Life and Vitality. Ideally the bed should be in a position that enables you to see who is entering or leaving the room; behind the door it is vulnerable, and directly opposite the door it is subject to the force of incoming energy. There is a light covered by a lampshade to the side of the bed; if this was a bare bulb the glare could be harsh and disruptive. Lights above the head of the bed should be avoided, as bright lights may cause headaches or their effects result in disturbed sleep. The weak areas on the right-hand side of the room can be improved through the elemental combinations above, but it is important not to disturb the flow of ch'i entering the room by hanging a mirror at the end of the wardrobe directly in line with the door or on the front of the wardrobe opposite the foot of the bed. The space in front of the door has been left clear so ch'i entering the room can flow evenly and circulate freely.

Productive cycle	Destructive cycle
wood produces fire	wood destroys earth
fire produces earth	earth destroys water
earth produces metal	water destroys fire
metal produces water	fire destroys metal
water produces wood	metal destroys wood

The Bathroom

The bathroom and lavatory are a source of germs, and the sha that accumulates here could spread into the areas where you eat, rest or sleep. Adequate ventilation is important to prevent the build-up of negative energy. Although the bathroom can be positioned on any side of the house, the door should not open directly on to the kitchen, bedroom or living room. If at all possible, the bathroom should definitely not be sited at the centre of the house or apartment, since germs could easily circulate to all parts of the house.

The bathroom door should not be close to the front door (top left), since the yin spirits of the bathroom clash with the yang spirits entering the house. The front door is the main access for ch'i into your home, and this flow could be disrupted by malign energy from the bathroom. Keep the bathroom door shut, particularly when the front door is open. Try to create positive feng shui conditions in the hall. If the bathroom is at the centre of the home (left), there is a risk that sha will easily travel to all the surrounding rooms. If you have a bathroom door that opens on to the kitchen, bedroom or living room (above), it is important to keep the door closed to prevent the spread of sha.

good feng shui   bad feng shui   improved feng shui

The bathroom door should not open directly on to the lavatory or bath, since these are the places where you need privacy and protection (above left). If it does, and if there is enough room in your bathroom, position a screen or panel in the space between the door and the toilet (above right). Avoid placing a mirror opposite the door since incoming ch'i will be directly reflected back.

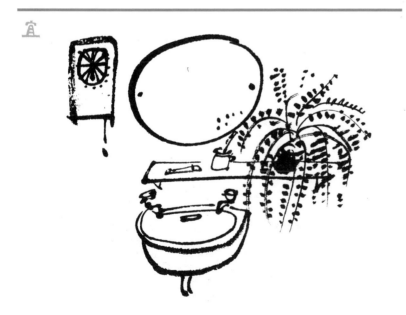

If there is no window in your bathroom you should instal a ventilation fan, as the adequate circulation of air is particularly important, since it prevents the accumulation of negative energy.

Checklist

• If there is no window, is there adequate ventilation and light in the bathroom?

• Is there any waste blocking the sink or are there waste-baskets left unemptied?

• Is the lavatory close to the front door, and if so, is the door kept shut?

• Does the lavatory door open directly on to the bedroom, kitchen or living room?

• Are there blinds, curtains or a screen to give you adequate privacy if needed?

The Dining Room

The dining room is a place for the family to relax, share conversation and entertain, but more importantly it is a room where food is consumed and where family decisions may be made. As such, it should not be too dark, cramped or unprotected. Sometimes this room is also used as a study or work area because the dining table is a useful place to spread out papers and books. In both cases, the room should not be subject to disturbing influences such as traffic noise or doors opening and closing, thereby disrupting the equilibrium of the room.

If there are doors leading in and out of the dining room, try to keep them closed when you are eating so you are not vulnerable to the flow of energy coming in one door and out of the other. This arrangement can make you feel nervous, hurried or unsettled.

If the table is close to patio doors or a window with very large glass panes, the food could be spoiled by sun or you may be subject to too much yin from cold or damp seeping into the room. Blinds or partly closed curtains will help to control these negative effects.

good feng shui   bad feng shui   improved feng shui

When the dining and living areas share the same room, try to define the two spaces. Separate them with a screen or other item of furniture like a bookcase. Once you have eaten you can then move to a separate place to relax.

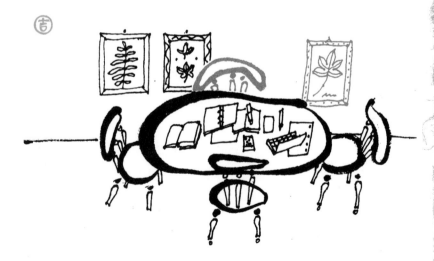

If you are using the dining room as a study area, choose a seat with a wall behind it. This will give you protection and also help you concentrate. There is added security if you are sitting in a position from which you can see who is entering or leaving the room.

Checklist
• Is the eating area separate from the area where you relax?
• Are there two doors in the dining room directly in line with each other?
• Is the dining table close to a large single pane or patio window?
• Is there direct access to a bathroom or lavatory from the dining room?
• Is there adequate lighting in the room?
• Is there a clear path between the kitchen and the dining room so that hot plates and bowls can be safely carried?

In the Workplace

The principles for feng shui in the workplace share many of the guidelines for a house or an apartment, but in this context there is an extra dimension to encourage a healthy flow of money. The site and design of your business is just as important as the commitment to, and efficiency of, the service it provides to customers or clients. If the business is badly sited or arranged, prosperity, health and profits may suffer. If you have positive feng shui in your home, this may help to support your business and vice versa, but weak feng shui in the workplace and at home needs corrective action.

In the following pages, positive sites and features are outlined, as well as suggestions of ways to remedy negative positions and counteract the effect of malign energy. When you are assessing a site it is important to take into account the nature of the surrounding area as well. If business is already flourishing in a certain area, this is a sign of active and successful ch'i. However, if the land around your workplace has sluggish ch'i, your productivity will inevitably be affected – even if the feng shui of your shop or office is positive.

How to Analyse Your Office Floor Plan

If you have a private office or study, you can do a personal reading for the layout of that room, or if you have space in an open-plan office you can take a reading for the area immediately around your desk. The example below deals with an open-plan office, and in this situation you should use the Pa Tzu compass that relates to the director, manager or owner of the business (*see pages 24–6*).

We have used Pa Tzu compass number 1 (*see right*) in the reading given below. The element for this compass is water. Work through the example and apply the same technique to your office floor plan using your personal Pa Tzu compass.

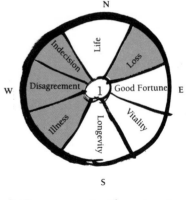

Pa Tzu compass 1 • Element: water

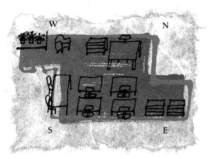

ABOVE *Scale drawing of office floor plan.*

BELOW *Overlaying your Pa Tzu compass on your floor plan.*

1 OVERLAYING YOUR COMPASS Draw a floor plan of your office to scale and overlay the relevant Pa Tzu compass, as explained on pages 26–7 (*see left and below left*). Remember to align north on the compass with the northern direction of the office. Alternatively, simply use the compass printed in this book and stand in the centre of the office, pointing north on the compass towards north in the office.

The Pa Tzu compass only has one element associated with it, but the eight directions of the room each have their own element. These directions and their associated elements do not change, regardless of where you are taking a reading.

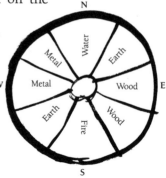

Directions and associated elements.

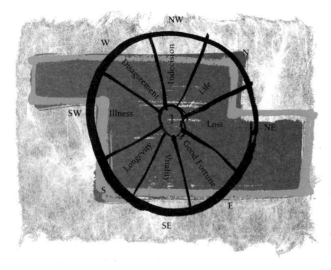

2 ASSESSING THE ELEMENTS You can see from our floor plan (*left*) that the four unlucky directions are in the west, north-west, south-west and north-east, and these are the areas that need attention. Since the element that belongs to Pa Tzu compass number 1 is water, you need to find water's relationship with metal and earth – the elements associated with the four unlucky directions in this example (*see floor plan on next page*). Look at the productive and destructive cycles of the elements shown opposite.

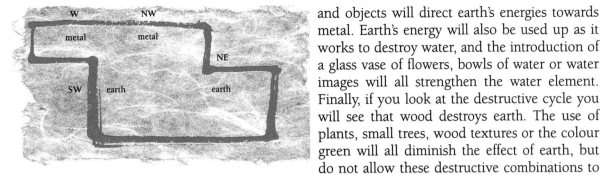

The unlucky directions and their associated elements.

3 WORKING THROUGH UNLUCKY DIRECTIONS Work through each of your unlucky directions and its relationship with your personal element – in this case, water – one step at a time.

☒ *West and north-west fall into the categories of Disagreement and Indecision. The element associated with both these directions is metal. The table below shows that metal produces water.*

This is a positive reading, since the two elements complement each other in the creative cycle. Although it is not necessary to take corrective action, the water element can be increased by the careful introduction of the colour black in office equipment or by hanging images that depict water. Another easy way to increase water is to add a vase of flowers, but make sure that the water does not become stagnant.

☒ *South-west and north-east fall into the categories of Illness and Loss. The element associated with both these directions is earth. The table below shows that earth destroys water.*

In order for water to gain strength the earth element has to be weakened by channelling it towards another element. Since earth creates metal, the introduction of metal colours, textures and objects will direct earth's energies towards metal. Earth's energy will also be used up as it works to destroy water, and the introduction of a glass vase of flowers, bowls of water or water images will all strengthen the water element. Finally, if you look at the destructive cycle you will see that wood destroys earth. The use of plants, small trees, wood textures or the colour green will all diminish the effect of earth, but do not allow these destructive combinations to become too powerful.

4 OFFICE LAYOUT The position of desks in an office is important for the productivity of the staff, but above all it is the director's desk that requires particular attention. If the desk belonging to the person who runs the company is in a weak position, the effects can reverberate at all levels of the company. It is also important for staff making financial decisions to be in a secure position where they are not subject to frequent disturbances or a sudden onrush of ch'i. In this example the director's desk is in the top right-hand corner, protected on two sides by a wall but not hemmed in by these walls. The person sitting here is able to see who is entering and leaving the office, yet is distanced enough from the door not to be subject to a surge of energy entering the room. The director's desk falls into the categories of Life and Indecision, but the elemental combinations above can help to improve the weak section. While most of the other desks in the office are positioned so that those seated at them have the support of a wall behind, the desks in the centre of the room do need additional support. The room containing the printers in the top left-hand corner is screened off to lessen the disruptive impact the noise may have on both the staff and the circulation of ch'i.

Productive cycle	Destructive cycle
wood produces fire	wood destroys earth
fire produces earth	earth destroys water
earth produces metal	water destroys fire
metal produces water	fire destroys metal
water produces wood	metal destroys wood

The Site of a Business

Your workplace should be sited according to the nature of the business you want to encourage. If you are dependent upon a regular flow of customers, then choose a thriving business area, which is evidence of active ch'i on that site. It is better to find small premises in a well-established district than large premises in a deserted area. If you rely on a peaceful environment for your work, choose a more residential area.

The building that houses your workplace should not be lower in height than neighbouring buildings, since the pressure they exert could affect your judgement and creativity. It should also be sited on raised ground to avoid flooding. Be alert to neighbouring structures or features such as the corners of roads or power lines that could cut through the circulation of ch'i and carry negative energy directly to your premises. You should also assess the buildings that are nearby to see if the four animal guardians are well-balanced, offering your workplace security and protection.

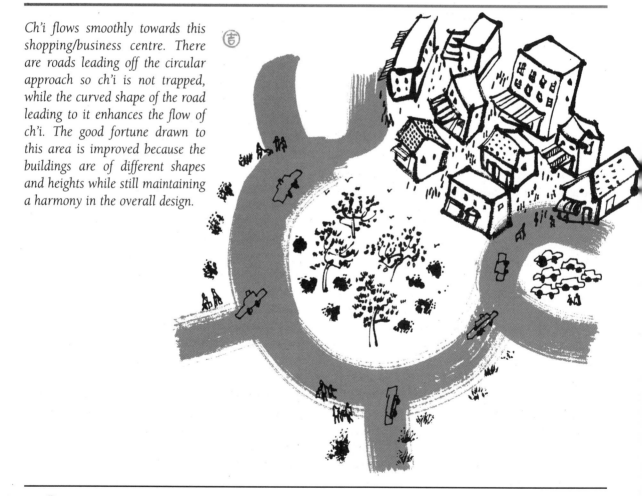

Ch'i flows smoothly towards this shopping/business centre. There are roads leading off the circular approach so ch'i is not trapped, while the curved shape of the road leading to it enhances the flow of ch'i. The good fortune drawn to this area is improved because the buildings are of different shapes and heights while still maintaining a harmony in the overall design.

good feng shui   bad feng shui   improved feng shui

The intersections of roads and roundabouts are usually busy areas that attract positive business ch'i. However, if the business is on the corner of a crossroads (below), the main entrance should not face one of the opposite corners. Try to move the entrance to the side or place a reflective object over the door to send back any negative forces directed at the building.

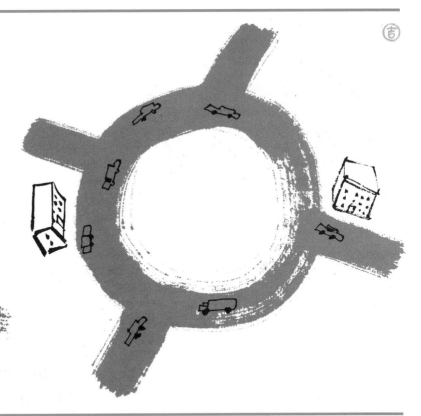

ABOVE A business should not be sited next to a road that has fast and heavy traffic. Ch'i is dispersed by the rapid movement of the vehicles, and the workers' sense of well-being is disrupted by noise and pollution levels. Use mirrors or springs to deflect or bounce back destructive forces. Ground-floor windows can also be shielded with blinds. The reading is improved if the site is back from the road and has a green area in front of it, producing healthy ch'i and providing space for clients or employees to walk or sit.

BELOW A quiet street with little traffic can adversely affect business, since the lack of activity deadens business ch'i. Attract attention by brightly decorating and signposting the front of the building. A sense of activity and energy can be created inside a shop with moving objects – fans, aquariums and small fountains. The site may prove productive if the business requires a quiet environment and is not dependent on attracting customers from the street.

The narrow gap between the two buildings siphons the profits away from the business facing it. The gap is likened to a thin slice taken out of a cake. (See advice on page 113.)

The corner of one building facing the main entrance of another has a negative effect, since it resembles a knife slicing into the profits of the business. (See advice on page 113.)

The bend of the road is likened to a scythe cutting into the business, weakening the productivity and harmony of the company. (See advice on page 113.)

When the road forks opposite the main entrance it can create confusion and disappointment, since the profits that should be directed into the building are being channelled away. (See advice on page 113.)

 good feng shui   ⊠ bad feng shui   盒 improved feng shui

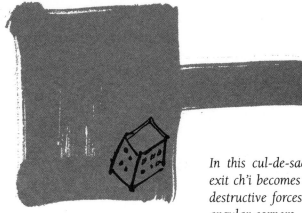

In this cul-de-sac with a narrow exit ch'i becomes trapped, causing destructive forces to gather in the angular corners. This weakens the efficiency of the business. Avoid positioning the front door opposite these points. (See advice right.)

• **Advice** *In the previous five examples, the main entrance to the business needs strengthening to ward off negative forces. Position a mirror so that destructive energy is sent straight back, or use reflective surfaces to deflect this energy (take care not to deflect it on to neighbours or back on yourself). Create a screen with blinds or a porch, or move the entrance to the side. Introduce greenery and lights to activate ch'i. Bounce away negative energy with a spring facing the dangerous corner of an overpowering structure.*

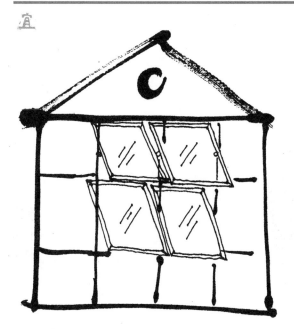

Windows are one way ch'i enters a building. Reflective glass limits or blocks ch'i; in turn, this limits the efficiency of those working inside. If windows cannot be opened to allow energy in, increase the circulation of ch'i inside with lights, plants, a fan or moving water.

If your business faces buildings or structures with a large area of reflective surfaces such as glass, polished steel or aluminium, try to block or fracture the reflections by adding features such as awnings, greenery or balconies.

If you are choosing a site, assess the natural and built features carefully. Avoid low-lying land and garbage depots where ch'i is stagnant and sha is present. These factors will adversely affect the health and efficiency of the staff.

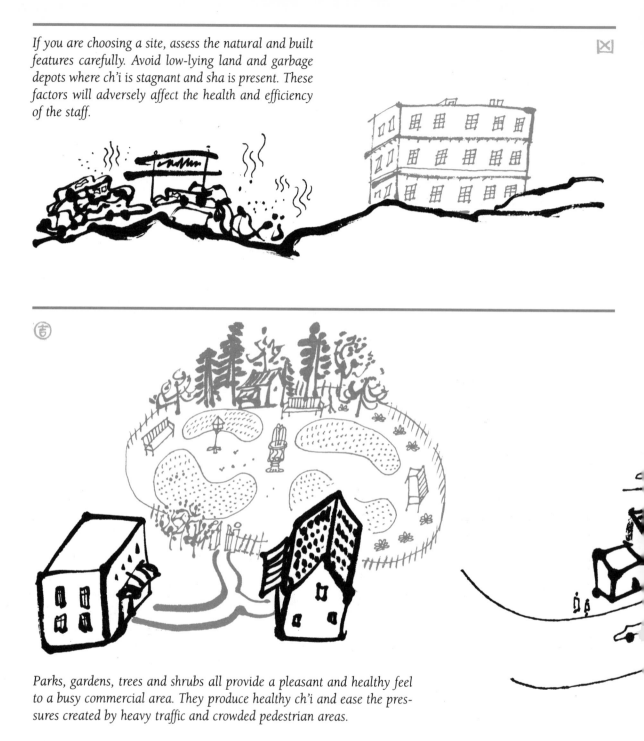

Parks, gardens, trees and shrubs all provide a pleasant and healthy feel to a busy commercial area. They produce healthy ch'i and ease the pressures created by heavy traffic and crowded pedestrian areas.

good feng shui   bad feng shui   improved feng shui

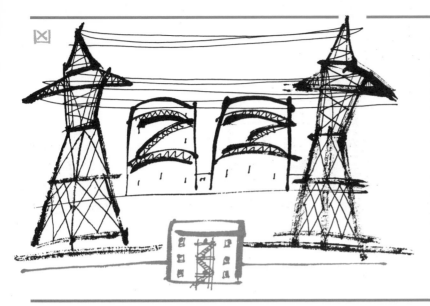

Beware of nearby power stations and derelict sites, and of satellite dishes and cables pointing at the building. Their impact can be bounced away with springs or a mirror; open scissors positioned above the mirror offer further protection by cutting through the effect of power cables. Sha that travels along power cables or from satellite dishes can also be absorbed with open trays or boxes of sand, wood chips or foam.

Although the shapes and sizes of buildings can differ in a busy commercial area, the overall planning, design and movement of traffic and people should have a basic harmony. Do not choose cramped, congested or dark sites.

Your workplace should not be dwarfed by other buildings, which act like oppressive weights, stunting the growth of your business. Place sword-like objects or springs on the roof to ward off destructive energy.

If the building on the Green Dragon side of your workplace is higher than your building, it should not have a detrimental effect, since the Green Dragon has an active and productive spirit.

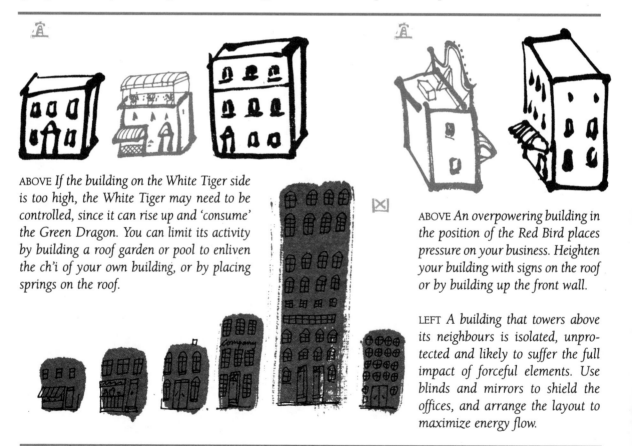

ABOVE *If the building on the White Tiger side is too high, the White Tiger may need to be controlled, since it can rise up and 'consume' the Green Dragon. You can limit its activity by building a roof garden or pool to enliven the ch'i of your own building, or by placing springs on the roof.*

ABOVE *An overpowering building in the position of the Red Bird places pressure on your business. Heighten your building with signs on the roof or by building up the front wall.*

LEFT *A building that towers above its neighbours is isolated, unprotected and likely to suffer the full impact of forceful elements. Use blinds and mirrors to shield the offices, and arrange the layout to maximize energy flow.*

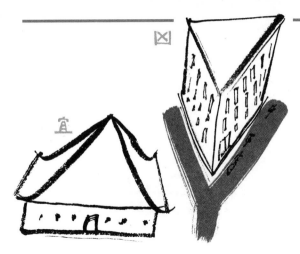

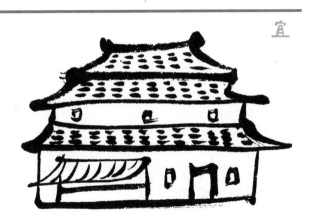

Triangular or blade-shaped premises trap destructive energy in their points, but curves help to soften this effect. This problem is difficult to avoid, so ensure internal energy flow is maximized.

Ch'i rolls quickly off layers or sloping roofs, which is an indication that business success will gradually slip away from you. Curved eaves will catch ch'i and control its flow.

A business needs solid foundations, which supporting pillars cannot provide. The ch'i in this building is also disturbed by the continual movement of the cars entering and leaving the car park. Lack of space means this problem cannot be eliminated entirely, but it can be improved by enlarging and rounding the pillars.

Top-heavy buildings lack support and can also oppress those working at lower levels. The weight from the higher levels may result in divisions being created within the company. The pressure can be alleviated by placing wide, and preferably round, pillars under the unsupported sides of the structure.

good feng shui   bad feng shui   improved feng shui

Entrance to the Workplace

The area in front of the workplace should be bright and welcoming and the path outside well paved and smooth. A blockage outside the main entrance could divert ch'i away into neighbouring businesses. Clear away waste bags and boxes, which are sources of sha, and make sure the entrance to the workplace is well-lit and clearly indicated. Avoid leading customers down dark or cramped pathways, since this means they will have passed through an area where ch'i is limited even before they have made a decision whether to buy your goods or use your services. A clean, bright, well-maintained entrance not only attracts beneficial energy but also creates a positive atmosphere for those who are about to conduct business there. If you rely on the public for your trade, it is particularly important that the main entrance is not obscured from public view.

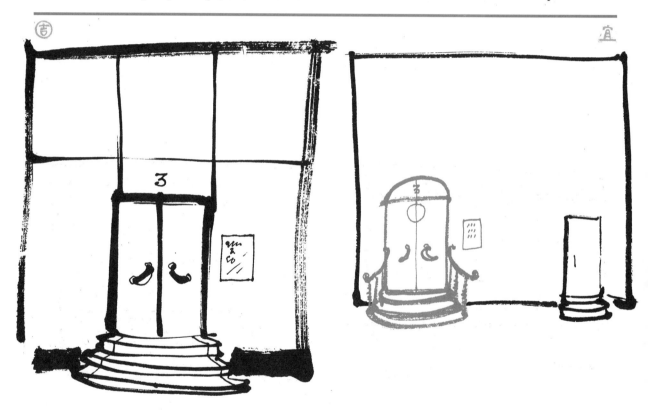

The main door of a business should be larger than that of a domestic residence to draw customers inside, and should be slightly higher than street level to limit negative forces entering. It should be wide and well-maintained to encourage ch'i and create a positive first impression; if the door is small, extra panelling or glass around the door can create the illusion of size.

Some premises have more than one entrance; in small businesses this can both confuse customers and divert ch'i. Ideally the main access point should be on the Green Dragon side of the building, since this side symbolizes activity. If this is not possible, you should still try to create a main access point by clearly marking one entrance and making it welcoming.

Ch'i is squeezed when it is channelled swiftly through a narrow porch or has to enter low, cramped doorways. Clear away clutter to maximize access for ch'i and keep a light on by the door or in the porch.

Cover or move drains and pipes at the front of the building since they are said to siphon away profits. The main drainage pipes should be at the side or, ideally, at the back of the building.

Large signs or vegetation hanging over the doorway obstruct the flow of beneficial business ch'i entering the premises. Move the sign above the doorway and cut back the vegetation.

Do not use materials or features that are pointed, angular or too rough. A façade of rough brick can, however, be used if it is constructed in an even, regular way on the frontage.

A steep flight of steps leading down from the entrance enables profits to roll out of the business. The steps should be graded less steeply and a porch built to prevent ch'i escaping. If this is not possible, make sure the door is kept shut and add an inner door to prevent loss of ch'i.

An awning over the main entrance helps to gather ch'i and channels it into the business. The awning should be in proportion to the overall size of the building or the entrance itself.

 good feng shui   bad feng shui   improved feng shui

Lobbies, Corridors and Doors

Once beneficial ch'i has entered your building, do not allow it to become trapped or diverted as a result of the conditions it immediately encounters. If the lobby, foyer or hallway is spacious, clean and bright, then there is a greater potential for ch'i to circulate freely. There should be several doors leading off the entrance area to allow for an increased flow of energy to various parts of the building, but avoid stairs or escalators located directly in front of the main entrance. In this position, they provide rapid access for negative forces to the upper floors of the building. Stairs or escalators also pull enriching ch'i away from the ground floor.

ABOVE The foyer should be wide, bright and welcoming with several doors or exits leading to other parts of the premises, allowing ch'i to circulate freely. Once ch'i has entered the business, it can become trapped in small dark foyers and will be further limited if there is only one door leading to the rest of the business. In cases such as this, always keep the area well lit.

 BELOW Do not block the circulation of ch'i into the building by putting heavy obstacles or furniture in the foyer or reception area. Make sure that waste-bins are emptied regularly and remove any rubbish bags to prevent the accumulation of sha.

Your prosperity will be affected if elevator doors face the entrance, since ch'i is rapidly channelled into the elevator preventing it from circulating on the ground floor. Similarly, stairs opposite the main entrance allow negative energy to gain easy access. A mirror can be used to reflect back some of the incoming energy, so it can travel in a different direction. If the entrance faces a lavatory, the door should be kept shut and the area screened with a reception desk or display counter to prevent sha unbalancing and dissipating incoming ch'i.

good feng shui   bad feng shui   improved feng shui

Bright colours, space, light and a reasonable amount of greenery or number of flowers enhance the feng shui of a lobby or reception area. The gentle movement of a fountain activates ch'i and draws good fortune in to the premises.

Avoid choosing an office that faces a steep staircase or an elevator, since financial fortune can easily slip away. Keep the door shut and erect a bookcase or screen inside the office to prevent excess ch'i escaping.

The flow of beneficial ch'i is limited to an office at the end of a long, narrow corridor, while negative forces can be directed like an arrow straight to your door. As a result, your authority or decision-making skills may be weakened. If you cannot change office, hang a small mirror above the door to reflect the oncoming energy.

A cooking and eating area should be screened off from the entrance, since the smells and noise are disruptive to clients. Exceptions are made for businesses connected with catering.

If offices lead off a long wide corridor, the corridor should be well-lit, bright and clean. Make sure the access to office doors is clear and that discarded files are removed and waste-baskets emptied regularly.

Workplace Layout

The position of your desk can affect your concentration, creativity and productivity, so you need to find conditions to suit your style of working and the nature of your work. If you are making crucial decisions or keeping accounts you are advised to sit in a quiet room, away from the main entrance, computer printers, the canteen and any other sources of noise that may disrupt your concentration. If you rely on group work then you may find that it is more conducive to be in a busy, lively office in order to encourage creativity.

The place where you sit needs good lighting and adequate ventilation to enliven ch'i. It also needs support: walls, screens or a piece of furniture behind your chair will offer protection. Try not to put yourself in a vulnerable position, whether it is in the direct line of an open door, escalator, flight of stairs or next to a large single-pane glass window, as this will affect your work.

RIGHT *The entrance to the manager's or accounts office should be well-lit, spacious and clear of rubbish, since these areas are at the heart of the business. A mistake here could weaken the 'limbs' of the business. If these offices are near the lavatory, an ornamental mirror over the door and a healthy plant nearby should prevent sha spreading.*

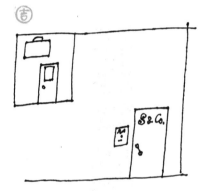

ABOVE *Unless the proprietor or director needs regular contact with customers, the director's office should not be seen by the public, since privacy and a quiet atmosphere aid concentration.*

LEFT *If the manager or director shares an open-plan office, his or her desk should be the focal point and situated in the strongest position. The other desks should be arranged evenly around the main desk, allowing for a smooth flow of ch'i through the room.*

When you are sitting at a desk your back needs support. A wall is ideal, since it offers both security and protection. (If you are unable to have your desk in this position you should follow the advice given in the caption to the right.)

A window or open door behind you is known as 'the empty door' and your concentration may slip through this space. If you cannot reposition your desk, create a shield with plants, filing cabinets or a bookcase (do not allow files or books to jut out above your head).

Avoid facing the door, since the incoming ch'i or malign energy can be too powerful, making it difficult for you to focus on your work or make decisions. In situations such as this, a vase of flowers, a rack for filing papers and a desk lamp would offer a level of protection.

If you are sitting with your back to the door, you can never be sure who is entering or leaving the room. A small mirror on the wall beside or in front of you will enable you to see what is happening behind you and help you feel more in control.

good feng shui   bad feng shui   improved feng shui

The desk in the corner on the opposite side of the room to the door is in the strongest position, with support at the back and a clear view of who is entering the room without being in direct line of the door. The desk on the right is protected at the back but does not immediately enable the person sitting there to see who is entering.

Desks that are positioned haphazardly and surrounded by clutter create a sense of confusion as well as disrupting the flow of ch'i over and around the features in the room. Clear the clutter and rearrange the desks to create a more harmonious and balanced working environment.

Many of the people sitting at the desks in this open-plan office are in a vulnerable position, since they have no support behind them and/or are unable to see who is entering the room. The tall screen between the desks slices through the ch'i and creates a feeling of oppression for those directly facing it, and should be removed or reduced in size. The desks that have the support of a wall, yet still afford a view of movement in and around the office, are better protected. The photocopier and printers in the centre should be screened off to lessen noise that cuts through the ch'i of the office.

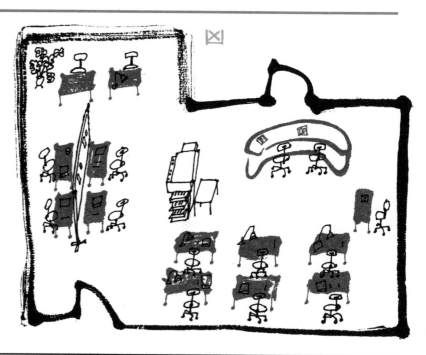

good feng shui   bad feng shui   improved feng shui

You can improve weak readings by adding protection in certain areas — for example, keeping a blind down to add support to your back, creating a low screen with a bookcase or cupboard, introducing greenery or flowers, and installing bright but not overpowering lights. Small reflective objects will also help to send back negative energy. Finally, you can move your desk to an angle to avoid backing on to weak areas.

If the business is a shop or restaurant, the position of the tills is especially important. These should be located at a busy point, to encourage the flow of money, but should not face an entrance or doorway, since the money will flow out as readily as it enters.

Checklist

• Can ch'i circulate freely in and around the office furniture?
• Are waste-baskets emptied regularly and discarded files removed?
• Do you have support or protection when you are sitting at your desk?
• Can you see who is entering or leaving your office or study?
• Does your desk face an open door?
• Is there a window directly behind your chair?
• Is your desk in a dark corner of the office?
• Are you sitting next to noisy computers or other office equipment?
• Is access to the office cramped, poorly lit or narrow?
• Is the accounts office in a quiet and well-protected area?

Bibliography and Further Reading

de Bary, Theodore (editor), *Sources of Chinese Tradition Vol. I.* New York, NY: Columbia University Press, 1960.

Kwok, Man-Ho, *The Feng Shui Kit: The Chinese Way to Health, Wealth and Happiness, at Home and at Work.* Edited by Joanne O'Brien. First published in 1995 by: Piatkus, London; Charles E. Tuttle Co. Inc., Boston, MA; HarperCollins*Publishers*, Sydney; Asiapac Books, Singapore.

Kwok, Man-Ho, and Joanne O'Brien, *The Elements of Feng Shui.* Shaftesbury, England/Rockport, MA: Element Books, 1991.

Kwok, Man-Ho, Martin Palmer and Jay Ramsay, *The Illustrated Tao Te Ching.* Shaftesbury, England/ Rockport, MA: Element Books, 1993.

Legge, James (translator), *The Chinese Classics Vol. III.* Oxford: Oxford University Press, 1871 (reprinted by

Southern Materials Center Inc., Taipei, 1983).

Needham, Joseph (translator), *Science and Civilisation in China Vol. II.* Cambridge: Cambridge University Press, 1956.

Palmer, Martin, Jay Ramsay and Zhao Xiaomin (translators), *I Ching: The Shamanic Oracle of Change.* London/San Francisco, CA: Thorsons, 1995.

Palmer, Martin and Zhao Xiaomin, *Essential Chinese Mythology.* London/San Francisco, CA: Thorsons, 1997.

Wong, Eva, *Feng Shui: The Ancient Wisdom of Harmonious Living for Modern Times.* Boston, MA: Shambhala, 1996.

Wong, Eva, *The Teachings of the Tao.* Boston, MA: Shambhala, 1997.

Index
Page numbers in *italics* refer to illustrations

A

aerials 57
animal guardians 18–19, 40
  in garden 66
  in shape of home 68
  in topographical features 15–16, 40–2, *41*, *42*
apartments *see* homes

B

balance, re-establishing 6
balconies 57
bathroom 102–3, *102–3*
bedroom 96–9, *96–9*
  analysing floor plan 100–1, *100–1*
Bird, Red 18, *18, 19*, 34–5, 66, 116

Black Tortoise 18, *18, 19,* 66, 73
blinds 31
buildings, near houses 56–9, *56–9*

C

cemeteries 59, 115
change, process of 10
Ch'i 13
  flow 6, 32
  in landforms 15–16, *15*, 17, 38–53
chimneys 71
Chu Hsi 13
coastal waters 42
colours:
  elements and 22

  use in protecting site 30–1
conservatories 65
creation 11–12
curtains 31
curves 33

D

day centres, near homes 59
dining room 104–5, *104–5*
dragon 7
  Green, as guardian spirit 18–19, 66, 68, 116
  as landform 15–16, *15*, 41
dragon's blood 15

E

earth 15
  associations 21
  in cycles of elements 20
  in landforms *43*
  shape in watercourses 44, *44*
  union with heaven and humanity 10, *11*
electric pylons 47
elements 15, 20–3
  associations 21
  colour and 22
  cycles 20–1, *20*
  introducing into room 23
  in landforms 43–4, *43*
  personal 24–7
  use to improve feng shui

22–3
yin/yang and 21
emotions, change in 10
energy see ch'i
entrances:
 to homes 70, 70, 73–7,
  73–7
 to workplace 118–19,
  118–19
environment, relationship
 with 10

F
feng shui:
 meaning 6, 37
 principles 10–19
fire 15
 associations 21
 in cycles of elements 20
 in landforms 43
 shape in watercourses
  44, 44
fish 33
five elements see elements
Former Heaven 14
fountains 64
four animal guardians 18,
 40, 66, 68

G
garages 72
garbage see rubbish
gardens 64–7, 64–7
Green Dragon 18, 18, 19,
 66, 68, 116
guardians 18, 40, 66, 68

H
hall and stairs 82–3, 82–3
harmony, re-establishing 6
heaven, union with earth
 and humanity 10, 11
heaven ch'i 13
hills, interpreting 40–4
homes 37
 analysing plan 80–1,
  80–1
 driveways 74
 features surrounding
  54–77
 gardens 64–7, 64–7
 other buildings 56–9,

56–9
 plots of land 60–3,
  60–3
 front door 73–7, 73–7
 inside 78–105
 lights outside 71, 74
 porches 77
 porticoes 70
 roof shapes 69, 70, 71
 in rural landscapes 45–8,
  45–8
 shape 68–72, 68–72
household objects 31–2
houses see homes
Huai Nan Tzu 11–12
humanity, union with
 heaven and earth 10,
 11

I
I Ching 7
 trigrams 14, 14

K
kitchen 90–3, 90–3
 analysing floor plan
  94–5, 94–5
 open-plan 84, 84
knives 93

L
lakes 42
land:
 energy in 7
 plots around homes
  60–3, 60–3
landforms:
 animal forms in 15–16,
  40–2, 41, 42
 dragon as 15–16, 15
 energy 17
 five elements in 43–4, 43
landscape 37
 change in 10
 dragon seen in 15–16, 15
 interpreting 40–8
 rural 45–8
 union of heaven, earth
  and humanity 10, 11
 yin and yang in 12
Later Heaven sequence 14
lavatory 102–3

Li 13
lights 71, 74
living room 84–7, 84–7
 analysing floor plan
  88–9, 88–9

M
masts 57
metal 15
 associations 21
 in cycles of elements 20
 in landforms 43
 shape in watercourses
  44, 44
mirrors 28–9
 in home 83, 86, 91, 97,
  99, 103
 outside home 50, 52, 56,
  57, 58, 62, 65, 75
 outside workplace 113,
  115, 116
 in workplace 123
moon 12
mountains 12
 interpreting 40–4

N
negative energy, protecting
 site from 28–33

O
offices see workplace

P
pa kua mirror 29, 62, 75
Pa Tzu compass 7, 14,
 24–7, 79
 analysing apartment floor
  plan 80–1, 80–1
 analysing bedroom floor
  plan 100–1, 100–1
 analysing kitchen floor
  plan 94–5, 94–5
 analysing living-room
  floor plan 88–9, 89–9
 analysing office floor
  plan 108–9, 108–9
 Eastern Life 24, 25
 taking readings 27, 37
 using 26–7
 Western Life 24, 26
paths 67

patio 65
photographs 31
pictures 31
plant pots 67
playgrounds, in relation to
 homes 59
pools 64
porches 31
power lines 59, 115

R
Red Bird 18, 18, 19, 34–5,
 66, 116
rivers:
 interpreting 40–4
 shape of elements in 44,
  44
 yin and yang energy in
  13
roads 37
 patterns 49–53, 49–53
Roots digging deep into
 firm foundations 43,
 44
rubbish 67, 76, 120, 121,
 122
rural landscapes 45–8

S
satellite dishes 57, 115
schools, near homes 59
sculptures 31
seasons:
 change in 10
 heaven ch'i governing
  13
 yin/yang in cycle of 11,
  13
sha 13, 32
shrine 86
Shu Ching 15
site:
 choosing 42
 protecting 28–33
Snake, in landform 40–1,
 41
stairs 82, 83, 83
Submerged Dragon Swirls
 Tail 42
sun 12
Swan, in landform 40–1,
 41

swimming pools 65
symbols 31
symmetry 33

T

Tao 6–7, 10
textures 31
Tiger, White 18, *18, 19,* 66, 68, 116
Tortoise, Black 18, *18, 19,* 66, 73
trees 30
  behind house 66
  beside house 66
  between houses 48
  outside house entrance 76
  overshadowing house 66
trigrams 7, 14, *14*
  associations 14

on pa kua mirrors 29
personal 25, 26

V

vegetation, protecting site with 30

W

water 15
  associations 21
  in cycles of elements 20
  energy in 7
  flow in mountains 16
  garden pools 64
  in landforms *43*
  in landscape:
    shape of elements in 44, *44*
  yin and yang 12
  protecting site with 32–3
  shape in watercourses

44, *44*
Water Dragon 41
Water Dragon Classic 41, 44
White Tiger 18, *18, 19,* 66, 68, 116
wind, flow 17, *17*
wind chimes 33, *33,* 59, 82, 93, 115
wood 15
  associations 21
  in cycles of elements 20
  in landforms *43,* 44
  shape in watercourses *44*
workbook, using 6–7, 36–7
workplace 37, 106–25
  analysing floor plan 108–9, *108–9*
  corridors 120–1, *121*
  doors 120–1, *120*

entrance 118–19, *118–19*
layout 122–5, *122–5*
lobbies 120–1, *120–1*
siting 110–17, *110–17*
worship, places of, near homes 59
wu xing see elements

Y

yang-domain animal formation 18, *19*
yin-domain animal formation 18, *18*
yin/yang 11–12
  balance 6
  elements and 21
  interaction and tension 14
  movement 7
  opposite forces 12, 15
  symbol *11*

Acknowledgements

AUTHOR'S ACKNOWLEDGEMENTS

We would like to thank our colleagues and friends at ICOREC for their invaluable support and advice during the preparation of this book. We would also like to express our gratitude to Tessa Monina, Sarah Howerd and illustrator, Meilo So.

EDDISON • SADD EDITIONS

Editorial Director	Ian Jackson
Editor	Tessa Monina
Proofreader	Nikky Twyman
Indexer	Dorothy Frame
Art Director	Elaine Partington
Senior Art Editor	Sarah Howerd
Illustrator	Meilo So
Chinese Calligrapher	Hing-Bun So
Production	Karyn Claridge and Charles James

Also from the publishers of *The Feng Shui Workbook:*
THE FENG SHUI KIT by Man-Ho Kwok

The Feng Shui Kit contains a feng shui compass with ruler markings and a pa kua mirror, plus an illustrated instruction book.